WHAT IS
YOGA?

YOGA

FOR YOUR MIND AND BODY

A Teenage Practice for a
Healthy, Balanced Life

by Rebecca Rissman

SWITCH PRESS

TABLE OF
CONTENTS

What kind of girl do you want to be—fit, strong, smart, or chill? Look no further. You don't need to go to gyms or fitness centers that are filled with high-tech exercise machines. You don't need to wear a tiny computer on your shoe to record running distance and speed. You can become everything you want to be by doing one very low-tech activity—yoga.

Yoga is an ancient practice that comes from India. It involves working on the physical body, the mind, and the spirit through careful practice and determination. The word "yoga" comes from the Sanskrit word *Yuj*, which means "to unite, or join." Many people who practice yoga believe it helps them to unite and balance their body, mind, and spirit.

Yoga has many benefits. Some people practice yoga because it helps them feel less stressed or anxious. Others use yoga to improve their flexibility and strength. Yoga can even boost your brainpower. Whatever your goals, yoga can help you achieve them. Get ready to become the girl you've always wanted to be.

Asana

Pronounced: AH-sah-nah

From the root word *as*, meaning "to sit," or "to be"

Asana is a word you'll hear over and over during your yoga practice. This Sanskrit term is used to describe a yoga pose. Most yoga poses are named after animals, objects, or familiar motions. For example, ustrasana means "camel pose." Ustra is the Sanskrit word for "camel."

Today's fitness experts are starting to focus on one low-tech practice: yoga.

Many people who practice yoga believe it helps them to unite and balance their body, mind, and spirit.

As with any exercise or activity, having the right gear can help make your experience better. Yoga mats, blocks, bolsters, eye pillows, straps, and yoga blankets can all help you get more out of your yoga sessions.

Yoga Mats

One helpful yoga prop is a yoga mat. It is a long, thin rectangle made of a sticky material such as rubber. Yoga mats are useful because they can help keep your hands and feet from slipping when you get sweaty. You can certainly do yoga without a yoga mat, though. Any flat surface will do, as long as it's not slippery.

Blocks

Yoga blocks are simple but useful yoga props. These rectangular blocks are usually made of wood or foam and can be used to shorten a stretch or provide support. They can also be used to help keep your body in correct, safe alignment in yoga poses.

If it's hard for you to reach the floor in a standing pose without straining or feeling pain, use a block. Place the block under your fingertips to reduce the intensity of a stretch and prevent possible injury.

Bolster

Yoga bolsters are a bit like extra firm pillows. You can use bolsters to get more comfortable in seated postures, to boost your back in laying poses, and to help make some back-bending postures more comfortable. You can even use a bolster as a pillow in some reclining poses.

Eye Pillow

Eye pillows are helpful props to have on hand during Corpse Pose. These small rectangles of fabric are usually filled with rice, seeds, or beans. Sometimes they are even filled with scented herbs. If you're having trouble relaxing in Corpse Pose, place an eye pillow over your eyes when you lie down. The gentle pressure of the pillow over your eyes will help you relax.

Yoga Strap

A yoga strap is a simple but useful yoga prop. Yoga straps can be used to help modify poses. They can help you extend your reach if you're not quite flexible enough to perform the full version of a pose. For example, if you're not able to touch your toes in a forward fold, hook the strap across the balls of your feet and enjoy the stretch.

Yoga Blanket

Yoga blankets are thick, soft props that can be useful in many different poses. Folded, rolled, or laid flat, yoga blankets can be used to make poses easier or more comfortable. Fold a yoga blanket into a long rectangle and place it under your forehead in Extended Puppy Pose for a slightly easier version of this stretch.

CALM GIRL

Feeling Stressed?

Stop biting your nails and put down that stress ball. There's a better way to deal with anxiety that won't wreck your manicure. Why not give yoga a try? It's the ultimate workout for any super-stressed girl.

Yoga is a great activity to turn to when you feel overwhelmed. It combines controlled breathing, physical poses, and meditation to help you calm down and save your cuticles. Even after a short yoga practice, you'll be feeling more serene.

Most types of yoga will help you chill out, but some are specifically geared toward stress relief. If you want to move through different relaxing poses slowly, enjoying each one for several minutes, try Yin Yoga. It has a slow pace and focuses on alignment. If you want something a bit more active, try Restorative Yoga.

Some yoga poses are especially helpful when you need to calm down. Poses that allow you to sit or lie down are great for stress relief. So are gentle twists. Try to add these into your yoga practice the next time you can't stop your thoughts from racing.

Make Your Yoga Sessions
PEACEFUL

Quick—you rush out of your tutoring session, grab your gym bag, and sprint to your mom's car. You have 30 minutes to squeeze in a quick yoga practice in your bedroom before dinner.

If this sounds like you, you're probably going to have a hard time relaxing when you finally roll out your yoga mat. And who wouldn't? You can't rush, rush, rush, and then expect to suddenly chill out.

In order to make your yoga practice as relaxing as possible, follow these tips:

- Slow down! You might not have time for an hour-long yoga practice, but any amount will be helpful. Focus on being calm and steady. Try to be relaxed as you set up your mat, props, and water for your practice.

- Turn off your cell phone. You won't be as relaxed if you're worried it will ring, or if you're thinking about who might be texting you.

- Ask your family to give you privacy during your yoga practice. Knowing that nobody will barge in on you will help you relax.

- Play calm, quiet music that soothes you.

10

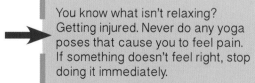

You know what isn't relaxing? Getting injured. Never do any yoga poses that cause you to feel pain. If something doesn't feel right, stop doing it immediately.

GET
WARMED up

Some people react to stress by tightening or tensing some of their muscles. When you do a variety of yoga poses, you will be able to release any muscle tension you might have.

Warming up your muscles before you stretch them will help you avoid becoming injured. This is why it's important to do strength-building yoga poses at the beginning of your practice. Lunges, squats, and poses that work your core are all great ways to get warm.

In addition to helping you relax tight muscles, the physical practice of yoga also helps you to release nervous energy. Do you ever feel like your heart is racing, and you can't calm down? If so, yoga can be a great way to blow off some steam.

When you're practicing yoga, make sure to do standing poses, seated poses, twists, and forward folds. If any areas of your body feel particularly tight, spend extra time on poses that work and stretch those areas. After you've worked up a good sweat and relaxed some of your muscles, you'll have an easier time relaxing and de-stressing.

Ever notice that you've got a stiff neck or painful lower back during a stressful time in your life? Yoga could be just what the doctor ordered.

LOCUST POSE

Sanskrit Name: *Salabhasana*
Pronounced: shah-lah-BAHS-ah-nah

Do you hold tension in your back when you get stressed? If so, you might feel some slight back pain or discomfort when you're doing something that makes you anxious. Alternating Locust Pose with belly rests is a great way to work and relax the muscles in your back, neck, and legs.

step 1 Lie on your belly with your arms down along your sides.

step 2 Bring your forhead down onto the mat. Have your hands resting on the mat with your palms facing up and your thumbs touching your outer thighs. Point your toes, and allow the tops of your feet to rest on the mat.

Point your toes.

step 3 Lift your head, chest, and legs away from the floor. Keep your legs very straight.

step 4 Pull your shoulders away from your ears as you lift your hands up off the mat. Point your fingers toward your lifted heels to lengthen the arms.

step 5 Look slightly upward. Hold for a few breaths.

step 6 Slowly lower all the way down onto your mat. Turn your head to rest your right ear down onto the mat. Take a few restful breaths.

step 7 Repeat a few times, resting the oposite ear down onto the mat each time.

➡️ If looking upward feels painful or uncomfortable, modify this pose by looking straight ahead or down at your mat.

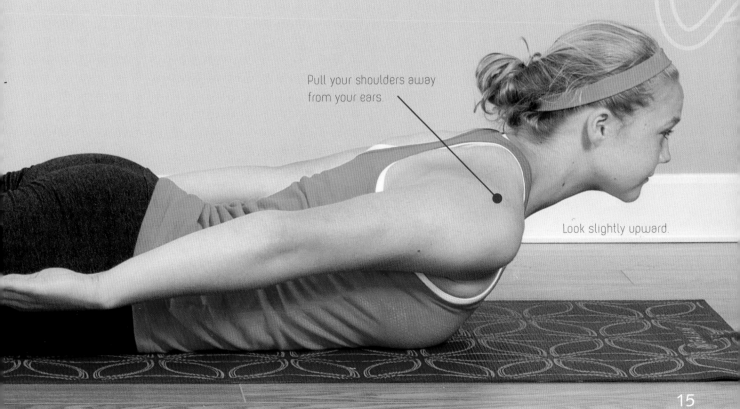

Pull your shoulders away from your ears.

Look slightly upward.

HALF-FROG POSE

Sanskrit Name: *Ardha Bhekasana*

Pronounced: ARE-duh bay-KAHS-ah-nah

Half-Frog Pose stretches the muscles in your legs, back, and abdomen. Hold this pose while focusing on your breath and alignment. Try your best to stay focused in Half-Frog Pose. If you get distracted, close your eyes.

step 1 Lie on your belly on your mat.

step 2 Bring your legs together, and point your toes.

Point your elbow up.

Press into your forearm to lift your chest and shoulders up.

step 3 Bring your right elbow under your right shoulder to press up into a small backbend. Then keep your elbow where it is as you bring your right hand under your left shoulder with your palm facing down. This will make your right forearm parallel to the top of your mat.

step 4 Bend your left knee. Reach back with your left hand to grasp the inner edge of your left foot. Pull your foot toward the left side of your bottom. If you are able to, turn your left hand so that your fingers point forward and your palm presses into the top of your left foot with your elbow pointing up.

step 5 Press into your right forearm to lift your chest and shoulders farther away from the mat. Square your shoulders by pressing your left shoulder forward and pulling your right shoulder back. Drop your shoulders away from your ears.

step 6 Slowly let go of the left foot. Return to your belly to rest.

step 7 Repeat on the other side.

If this stretch feels intense, don't worry about bringing your foot close to your bottom. Instead, keep your arm straight.

WARRIOR 2

Sanskrit Name: *Virabhadrasana*
Pronounced: vee-rah-bah-DRAS-ah-nah

Warrior 2 Pose works your legs, arms, and back. In many yoga classes, teachers challenge students to hold this pose for several breaths at a time. When you are holding Warrior 2 Pose, it's easy to allow your mind to wander to worries or stresses in your life. Resist this by focusing on your alignment and breathing.

Keep your arms parallel to the ground.

step 1 From a standing position, take a big step forward with your left leg. Point your left toes straight ahead.

step 2 Bend the left knee deeply while you keep your right leg as straight as you can. Turn your right heel down so that your whole foot is touching the mat.

step 3 Turn your hips to face the right side of your mat.

step 4 Extend your arms out to your sides, with your palms facing down. Pull your shoulder blades together and down your back to make space between your shoulders and your ears.

step 5 Look out over your left thumb.

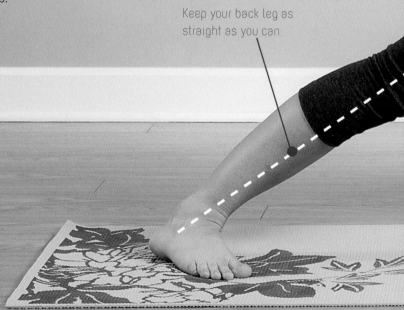

Keep your back leg as straight as you can.

step 6 Hold this for several breaths. Keep the deep bend in your left knee and focus on keeping your right leg very straight and strong.

step 7 Repeat on the other side.

Your front knee should hover right above your front ankle in this pose.

REVERSE WARRIOR

Reverse Warrior is a pose that often follows Warrior 2 Pose. It has all the benefits of Warrior 2, but with an additional deep side stretch that will really help release tension. Try flowing, or moving gracefully, between Warrior 2 and Reverse Warrior. Exhale into Warrior 2 Pose, and inhale into Reverse Warrior. Make each movement last as long as your breath. You can do this as many times as you like.

Face your palm to the floor.

Look up.

step 1 Start in Warrior 2 Pose with your left foot forward.

step 2 Flip your left palm in to face your body.

step 3 Bring your right hand down to the outside of your right thigh and reach your left hand straight up.

step 4 Slowly start to slide your right hand farther down your right leg. Reach your left arm toward the back of your mat to deeply stretch your left side.

step 5 Look up.

step 6 Return to Warrior 2 Pose.

step 7 Flow between these two poses several times.

step 8 Repeat on the opposite side.

If the back bend in Reverse Warrior feels too intense, extend your left arm straight up.

SEATED WIDE-ANGLE FORWARD FOLD

Sanskrit Name: *Upavistha Konasana*
Pronounced: OOH-pah-veesh-tah cone-AHS-ah-nah

Seated Wide-Angle Forward Fold stretches your legs, back, pelvis, and hips. It's important to keep your mind focused on your alignment. If you relax too much in this pose, you could overstretch your muscles and potentially become injured. Focusing on your alignment will also clear your mind of any other thoughts.

step 1 Sit on your mat with your legs outstretched.

step 2 Separate your legs as wide as you can while keeping your hips angled slightly forward. To do this, arch your back and point your tailbone slightly out behind you.

step 3 Flex your feet, and point your toes and kneecaps straight up.

step 4 Bring your fingertips just in front of your hips on the mat. Straighten your back by lifting the crown of your head straight up.

step 5 Keep your feet flexed and your hips still. Very slowly, walk your fingertips forward until you feel a stretch in your pelvis, legs, and back. You might not walk your fingers very far forward—don't worry. Just find a position that feels challenging for you.

step 6 Hold for a few breaths.

step 7 Slowly walk your hands back in toward your body to come out of this pose.

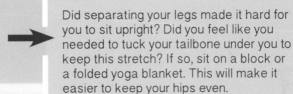

Did separating your legs made it hard for you to sit upright? Did you feel like you needed to tuck your tailbone under you to keep this stretch? If so, sit on a block or a folded yoga blanket. This will make it easier to keep your hips even.

Point your kneecaps straight up

Flex your feet

23

SEATED WIDE-ANGLE FORWARD FOLD VARIATIONS

Once you've learned the basics of Seated Wide-Angle Forward Fold, you can have fun playing with different variations of it. The twisted version is a nice way to stretch the spine and low back. For an invigorating abdominal stretch, try the side-opening version.

TWISTED SEATED WIDE-ANGLE FORWARD FOLD

step 2

step 1 Start in Seated Wide-Angle Forward Fold.

step 2 Sit up very tall by lifting the crown of your head up. Pull your belly button in toward your spine.

step 3 Bring your hands to either side of your right thigh. Point your belly button toward your right kneecap.

step 4 Keep your back as straight as you can, and keep both feet flexed with your toes pointing up. Walk your hands toward your right foot. Stop when you feel challenged.

step 5 Hold for a few breaths.

step 6 Walk your hands back in toward your hips to rest.

step 7 Repeat on the other side.

24

SIDE OPENING SEATED WIDE-ANGLE FORWARD FOLD

step 2

step 1 Start in Seated Wide-Angle Forward Fold.

step 2 Sit up very tall by lifting the crown of your head up. Pull your belly button in toward your spine.

step 3 Lift your right hand up.

step 4 Bring your left hand to the mat in front of you.

step 5 Turn your chest open to the right. Begin to stretch the right side of your body by reaching your right hand toward the left.

step 6 Hold for a few breaths.

step 7 Repeat on the other side.

TWISTED HEAD-TO-KNEE POSE

Sanskrit Name: *Parivrtta Janu Sirsasana*
Pronounced: pahr-VREE-tah JAH-new seer-SAHS-ah-nah

Are you ready for more of a challenge? Twisted Head-to-Knee Pose takes the stretch you got in the previous pose and adds a bind and hip stretch. Try this pose after you've worked on Side Opening Seated Wide-Angle Forward Fold to get the maximum benefits.

step 1 Start in a seated position with your legs outstretched.

step 2 Bring your left heel into the inside of your left thigh. Allow your left knee to fall out to the left.

step 3 Open your right leg out to the right as far as you can. Keep your right leg straight, and turn your right toes and kneecap up.

step 4 Bring your right forearm down onto the mat on the inside of your right shin, with your palm facing up.

step 5 Lift your left arm straight up.

step 6 Twist your chest open to the left.

step 7 Start to reach your left arm up and over toward your right foot. If you can, try to grasp your right big toe with your left hand. Grasp the inner edge of your right foot with your right hand as well. Holding the right foot with one or both hands is a bind.

step 8 Hold for a few breaths.

step 9 Repeat on the other side.

If you can't reach your left hand to your right foot, don't worry. Just think about turning your chest open and stretching your left side.

LEGS UP THE WALL POSE

Sanskrit Name: *Viparita Karani*

Pronounced: vee-pah-REE-tah car-AHN-ee

Inversions are yoga poses that bring the head below the heart. Most of the time, we think of poses like handstands and headstands as inversions. However, Legs Up the Wall Pose is a relaxing inversion that can help you de-stress.

step 1 Set a yoga bolster on your yoga mat about 6 inches (15 centimeters) away from a wall that doesn't have any shelves, pictures, or windows that you might bump. If you don't have a bolster, you could try using a pillow or a rolled-up blanket or sweatshirt.

step 2 Carefully lay your low back onto the bolster with your legs up the wall. This will take a little maneuvering. Scoot closer to the wall until your bottom is resting up against it. Your head and shoulders should comfortably rest on the mat.

step 3 Bring your feet together on the wall. Straighten your legs as much as you can.

step 4 Extend your arms out to the sides with your elbows bent and palms facing up.

step 5 Pull your shoulders down away from your ears. Gently rock your head from side to side to release any tension from your neck.

You might need to shift the bolster closer to the wall, or you might want to have it a bit farther away. Take a few minutes to get comfortable.

step 6 Close your eyes and be as still as you can.

step 7 Hold this position for several breaths.

step 8 Roll to one side to come out of this pose. Rest on your side for a few breaths.

VARIATIONS ON LEGS UP THE WALL POSE

If you love the Legs Up the Wall Pose, you might want to try a few variations on it. You can do many different leg positions in this pose. Just remember to rest on your side when you finish. Spending an extended amount of time with your legs raised could make you dizzy.

BOUND ANGLE VARIATION

step 1 Start in Legs Up the Wall Pose.

step 2 Bring the soles of your feet together, and allow your knees to fall to the sides.

step 3 Slide your feet down the wall toward your hips.

step 4 Using the muscles in your legs, press your knees toward the wall.

step 5 Hold for several breaths.

step 6 Return to Legs Up the Wall Pose, then rest on your side.

step 1

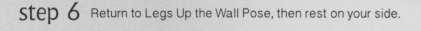

WIDE-LEGGED VARIATION OF LEGS UP THE WALL POSE

step 1 Start in Legs Up the Wall Pose.

step 2 Allow the legs to fall out to the sides until you feel a stretch in your pelvis.

step 3 Keep your feet flexed, and pull your kneecaps in toward your hips. Hold your legs where you feel the stretch, and breathe deeply.

step 4 Use your hands to help press your legs together to come back to Legs Up the Wall Pose. Then rest on your side.

step 1

Flex your feet.

31

HALF LORD OF THE FISHES POSE

Sanskrit Name: *Ardha Matsyendrasana*

Pronounced: ARE-duh mot-see-on-DRAHS-ah-nah

This twisting pose will definitely help you relieve stress. Many people hold muscle tension in their necks and shoulders. Half Lord of the Fishes Pose focuses on relaxing these tense areas.

step 1   Start in a seated position with your legs extended.

step 2   Bend your right knee up, and step your right foot just outside of your left knee.

step 3   Bend your left knee, and bring your left foot just outside of your right hip. This might take a bit of wiggling. Feel free to use your hands to get your foot in the right place.

step 4   Bring your right hand to the mat behind your hips. Straighten your right elbow, and sit up very tall.

step 5   Reach your left arm straight up. Make as much space as you can between your left ribs and your left hip.

step 6   Twist to the right, bringing your left elbow to the outside of your right knee. Turn your palm to face open to the right side of the mat.

step 7   Look over your right shoulder.

step 8   Hold for a few breaths and repeat on the other side.

If you aren't quite able to get your elbow to the outside of your knee, don't worry. A simple way to modify this pose is to hold the knee with your hand instead.

Keep your back straight.

MARICHI'S POSE

Sanskrit Name: *Marichyasana 3*
Pronounced: mar-ee-chee-AHS-ah-nah

Marichi's Pose looks a bit like Half Lord of the Fishes, but it stretches different areas. Remember to breathe deeply while doing Marichi's Pose. The deep twist and abdominal work, combined with slow and relaxed breathing, will have you feeling calm in no time.

Keep your back straight.

step 1 Start in a seated position with your legs extended.

step 2 Bend your right knee straight up, and pull your right heel as close into your right hip as you can.

step 3 Keep your left leg very straight. Flex your left foot so that your toes and kneecap point up.

step 4 Bring your right hand behind your hips. Straighten your right elbow.

step 5 Straighten your back as much as you can to sit up very tall. You will need to use your core muscles to do this. Pull your belly button in toward your spine, and reach up through the crown of your head.

step 6 Reach your left hand straight up into the air. Make as much space as you can between your left ribs and your left hip.

step 7 Twist to the right, bringing your left elbow to the outside of your right knee. Turn your palm to face open to the right side of the mat.

step 8 Look over your right shoulder.

step 9 Hold for a several breaths.

step 10 Repeat on the other side.

One of the hardest parts of this pose is keeping your back upright. Be patient and keep working on it.

Flex your feet.

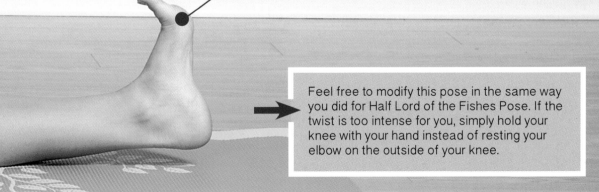

Feel free to modify this pose in the same way you did for Half Lord of the Fishes Pose. If the twist is too intense for you, simply hold your knee with your hand instead of resting your elbow on the outside of your knee.

WALL DOG POSE

Many people carry tension in their neck, shoulders, and upper back. This shoulder-opening pose encourages you to release tension in those areas. It is also a good stretch for the muscles in your legs. Try this pose when you need to take a break from your homework.

step 1 Stand facing a wall with no windows or objects hanging from it.

step 2 Place your palms on the wall shoulder-distance apart at the height of your elbows.

step 3 Walk your feet about 3 feet (1 meter) back away from the wall. Bend at the hips to bring your upper body horizontal. Keep your hips over your feet.

step 4 Press your hands into the wall until you feel a deep stretch in your shoulders.

step 5 Pull your belly button in toward your spine.

step 6 Keep your legs as straight as you can. Press into all parts of your feet.

Keep your back parallel to the ground.

Try not to let your upper body sag down toward the floor. Keep firm pressure in your hands to keep your upper body parallel to the floor.

CHILD'S POSE

Sanskrit Name: *Balasana*
Pronounced: bah-LAHS-ah-nah

Need a quick way to chill out? Do a few yoga poses to work and stretch your body, and then drop into Child's Pose for a few minutes. Before you know it, you'll feel less anxious and stressed. You might even feel a little sleepy.

step 1 Start on your hands and knees.

step 2 Bring your knees a bit farther apart and make your big toes touch.

Get comfortable. Experiment with having your knees closer together or farther apart until you feel as though you could stay in this pose comfortably. If your neck feels stiff, try rocking your head gently from side to side before becoming still with your forehead on the mat.

step 3 Sit your bottom down onto your heels and bring your forehead down to the mat.

step 4 Stretch out your arms in front of you. Lay your palms flat on the mat.

step 5 Press into your palms to straighten your elbows, and press your bottom into your heels.

step 6 Relax your upper body and allow your forearms to rest on the mat.

step 7 Hold for several breaths.

Don't be afraid to modify this pose. If your shoulders are especially tight, try resting your arms down along your sides. This modification will help lengthen and relax the muscles in your neck and shoulders.

Lay your palms flat on the mat.

RECLINED HERO'S POSE

Sanskrit Name: *Supta Virasana*
Pronounced: SOUP-ta veer-AHS-ah-nah

Reclined Hero's Pose stretches the muscles in your feet, hips, and thighs while allowing you to close your eyes and rest on your back. Try your best to relax the muscles in your jaw, shoulders, and low back while in this pose.

step 1 From your hands and knees, separate your feet so that they are slightly wider than your hips. Press the tops of your feet down into the mat.

step 2 Walk your hands back toward the outsides of your hips as you slowly sit between your heels.

step 3 Slowly, walk your hands behind you to begin to tilt your upper body back. With control, lower all the way onto your back. Do not allow your knees to lift away from the mat.

step 4 Press your tailbone forward.

step 5 Allow your hands to rest comfortably down at your sides.

step 6 Close your eyes and breathe deeply.

 Remember—don't do any pose that causes you pain. If the stretch described here feels too intense, stop at Step 2.

RECLINED BIG TOE POSE

Sanskrit Name: *Supta Padangusthasana*
Pronounced: SOUP-tah pah-dan-goose-TAHS-ah-nah

Are you ready for a rest? Reclined Big Toe Pose can be done standing or lying down. But don't be fooled! The reclined version is just as difficult—because you have to stay mentally balanced. Don't let your mind wander while doing this pose. Just think about your breath and alignment.

step 1 Lie on your back with your legs outstretched.

step 2 Loop your yoga strap around your right foot, and extend your right leg up. Hold the strap with your right hand. Straighten your right leg as much as you can.

step 3 Keep your left leg straight. Point your left toes and kneecap up. Press your left hip and heel into the mat.

step 4 Press your left hand down into the mat outside your left hip. Use your right hand to pull your right leg close to you. At the same time, press your right heel away from you. This will create muscular tension in the right leg.

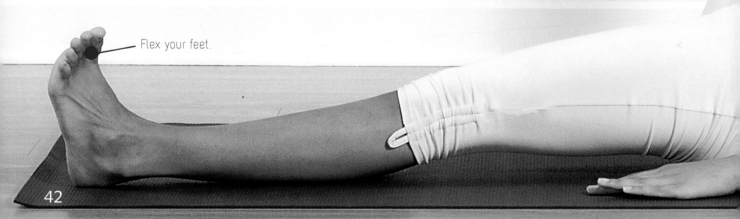

Flex your feet.

Are you super flexible? If so, drop the strap and hold onto your big toe with your thumb, index, and middle fingers.

step 5 Hold this for a few breaths.

step 6 Repeat on the other side.

VARIATIONS ON RECLINED BIG TOE POSE

Try these relaxing variations on Reclined Hand-to-Toe Pose. They stretch different parts of your hips, back, and legs. They are also a great way to wind down at the end of a challenging yoga workout. Just remember to keep your thoughts focused on the sound of your breath. Worrying about your homework won't help you de-stress.

HIP OPENING RECLINED BIG TOE POSE

step 1 Start in Reclined Big Toe Pose with your left leg extended into the air. Loop a yoga strap around your left foot, and hold it with your left hand. Be sure to keep both shoulders on the mat.

step 2 Press your right hand firmly down onto your right hip. Do not let your right hip lift away from the mat. Press all parts of your right leg down into the mat. Keep your right foot flexed, and point your right toes and kneecap straight up.

step 1

step 3 Slowly start to pull your left leg open to the left. You will feel this stretch in the left side of your groin. Keep your left leg as straight as possible, and flex your left foot.

step 4 When you feel this stretch becoming intense, stop and hold the pose. Take a few deep breaths.

step 5 Repeat on the other side.

CROSS-BODY RECLINED BIG TOE POSE

step 1 Start in Reclined Big Toe Pose with your left leg extended into the air. Loop a yoga strap around your left foot and hold it with your left hand. Press both shoulder blades into the mat.

step 2 Push your left hip into the mat. This will help lengthen the left side of your body.

step 3 Very slowly use your left hand to pull your left leg over to the right. Keep your left hip down on the mat. Your leg won't go very far over to the right, but you'll feel this stretch right away.

step 4 Repeat on the other side.

step 1

RECLINED TWIST

Sanskrit Name: *Supta Matsyendrasana*
Pronounced: SOUP-tah mot-see-en-DRAHS-ah-nah

A lot of people carry tension in their neck and back. Try to relax while you lie down and work out that tension. With Reclined Twist you'll enjoy the deep stretch in your neck, back, and as an added bonus, your legs.

step 1 Lie on your back with your legs outstretched.

step 2 Keep your left leg outstretched on your mat. Pull your right knee into your chest and give it a hug with both arms. Squeeze your knee in tightly.

step 3 Extend your right arm out onto the mat, palm facing down.

step 4 Use your left hand to pull your right knee to the left. If it's possible, bring the inside of your right knee to the mat outside your left hip.

step 5 Extend your left hand out onto the mat, palm facing down.

step 6 Turn your head to the right. Close your eyes and hold this for a few breaths.

step 7 Repeat on the other side.

Stack your hips.

RECLINED BOUND ANGLE POSE

Sanskrit Name: *Supta Baddha Konasana*

Pronounced: SOUP-tah BAHD-ah cone-AHS-ah-nah

Do you need to take a load off? Reclined Bound Angle Pose is a great way to chill out. Enjoy this calming, restorative pose for as long as you like. You can hold it for a few breaths or even while you take a short nap. Your hips, low back, neck, and shoulders will thank you for it.

step 1 Start out sitting. Bring the soles of your feet together, and let your knees fall to the sides.

step 2 Slide your feet closer to your body until you begin to feel a stretch in your hips. Don't worry about how close you can bring your heels into your body. This will be a different distance for everyone.

step 3 Slowly, lower your back down onto the floor.

step 4 Press your elbows firmly into the mat to briefly lift your upper body about an inch off the mat. With your back lifted, pull your shoulder blades closer together. Then relax onto your mat again. Your back should feel supported.

step 5 Extend your arms down at your sides. Have your palms face up.

step 6 Hold for several breaths.

If this pose feels too intense prop up your knees with bolsters or pillows. Doing this will reduce the intensity of the stretch.

HAPPY BABY POSE

Sanskrit Name: *Ananda Balasana*

Pronounced: on-ON-duh ball-AHS-ah-nah

Have you ever seen a baby happily playing with her feet? Channel your inner child in this carefree pose. Let yourself move and stretch in whatever ways feel good to you.

step 1 Lie on your back on your yoga mat.

step 2 Pull both of your knees into your chest. Hold the outsides of your knees with both hands and squeeze them tightly into your chest.

step 3 Keeping your knees close in to your body, extend your feet up.

step 4 Grasp the outer edges of your feet with your hands.

step 5 Pull your feet straight down toward the outer edges of your mat. Your knees will be splayed.

step 6   Get creative. Rock from side to side, or straighten one or both legs at a time. Feel free to explore this pose until you find a variation that feels good on your hips, legs, and back.

step 7   Stay in this pose for several breaths. Don't worry about holding still. If movement feels good in this pose, move.

Let your knees fall out to the sides of your body.

RECLINED PIGEON POSE

Between school, studying at home, and the occasional TV session, you probably spend a lot of time sitting. All that chair time can make your hips stiff. Try this relaxing pose to release tension from your hips and low back. Spend some time exploring how your body feels while you do this pose.

step 1 Lie down on your mat.

step 2 Bend your knees up and step your feet onto the mat just in front of your bottom.

Flex your feet.

step 3 Lift your left foot off the mat and cross it over your right knee. Try to rest the left ankle just outside the right knee. This will make this pose a bit more comfortable.

step 4 Flex your left foot so that the toes pull back toward the knee.

step 5 Lift your right foot off the mat, and pull your right knee in toward your chest.

step 6 Interlace your fingers on the back of the right thigh by bringing your left hand inside the leg and your right hand outside the leg.

step 7 Use the muscles in your left leg to press your left knee away from your chest. At the same time, use your arms to pull your right thigh closer to your chest.

step 8 Hold for a few breaths.

step 9 Repeat on the other side.

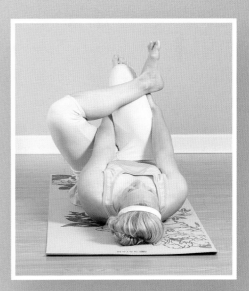

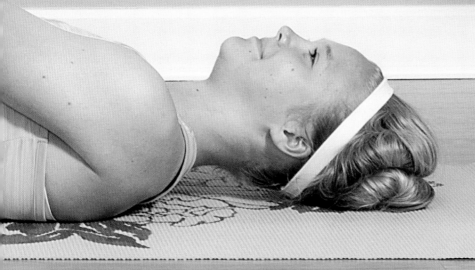

CORPSE POSE

Sanskrit Name: *Savasana*

Pronounced: sah-VAHS-ah-nah

You're brave. But are you brave enough to try something called Corpse Pose? Get comfortable. That's the most important rule for practicing Corpse Pose. You won't be able to fully relax if you're thinking about how your back is hurting, or if you need to take your hair out of your ponytail.

step 1 Get rid of anything that might distract you. If you're wearing glasses, take them off. If your hair is up in a tight or restrictive style, take it down.

step 2 Lie down onto your back.

step 3 Extend your legs out away from you. Separate your heels so that they are almost as wide as your mat.

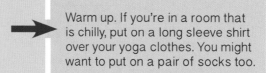

Warm up. If you're in a room that is chilly, put on a long sleeve shirt over your yoga clothes. You might want to put on a pair of socks too.

Corpse Pose is often done at the end of a yoga practice. However, feel free to do it whenever you need a little rest or relaxation!

step 4 Bring your arms down to your sides, palms facing up.

step 5 Adjust. Roll from side to side to get rid of any tightness in your back. Turn your head from side to side to release tension in your neck.

step 6 Relax. Release any tension from the muscles in your face and jaw. Drop your tongue away from the roof of your mouth.

step 7 Breathe deeply. Close your eyes. Try to become as still as possible.

step 8 Hold for several minutes.

step 9 Slowly roll to one side. Rest on your side for a few breaths before sitting up.

CORPSE POSE
continued

Corpse Pose is one of yoga's most important poses. In fact, some might say that Corpse Pose is the only pose that really matters. The goal of Corpse Pose is to achieve a state of mental and physical stillness. This is difficult to do because it's always tempting to scratch an itch or allow your mind to wander. But don't be discouraged. Use the lessons you've learned in your yoga practice to keep your mind focused on your breath instead of any distractions or worries. It won't be easy, but be patient.

Corpse Pose is traditionally done at the very end of a yoga practice. The fatigue you feel at that point will make it easier for you to completely relax. Corpse Pose can last from a few minutes to a half-hour or even more. Some yoga teachers might play music, chant, or sing during Corpse Pose. Others will keep the yoga room very quiet. Most people prefer to practice Corpse Pose in the dark. Allow your tired muscles to completely relax. Let your breath come naturally. Close your eyes. Do your best to ignore any ideas that pop up in your mind.

Experiencing tightness or pain in your low back while in Corpse Pose? Place a bolster under your knees when you lie down.

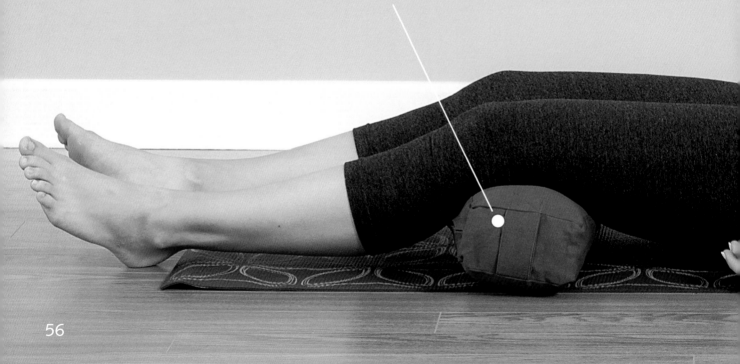

Eye Pillow

Eye pillows are helpful props to have on hand during Corpse Pose. These small rectangles of fabric are usually filled with rice, seeds, or beans. Sometimes they are even filled with pleasant-smelling herbs. If you're having trouble relaxing in Corpse Pose, place an eye pillow over your eyes when you lie down in this final posture. The gentle pressure of the pillow over your eyes will help you relax.

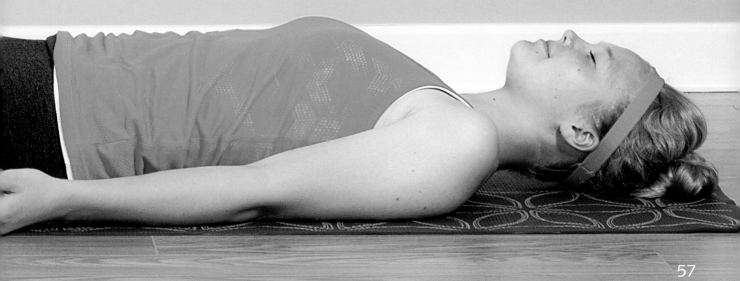

Relaxation
CHECKLIST

Feeling anxious about your test? Worried that you're being left out at school? Stressed about this Friday's big game? Follow these quick directions to help release some muscle tension:

- Unclench your jaw.

- Release the muscles in your shoulders.

- Relax the muscles in your low back.

- Gently rock your head from side to side to release the muscles in your neck.

- Drop your tongue away from the roof of your mouth.

Use Yoga to Stay Relaxed at School

Life is stressful. A girl like you can't always drop everything and hit her yoga mat to work through the latest drama. So how can you chill out on the go? It's easy. Just summon your yoga brain wherever you are.

Yoga teaches us to move slowly and carefully through different poses, focusing on our alignment and breath. Try to think this way about everything you do in life. Take things step-by-step. Whenever you feel overwhelmed, slow down and focus on your breath.

Yoga is more than just physical exercise. It's a way to exercise your brain and learn to control your thoughts. The more you work on staying focused and calm during yoga, the easier it will be to do in other areas of your life. Learning to take life one step at a time is one of the greatest benefits of practicing yoga.

Deep Breathing

Seeing red? Crazy stressed? Stop what you're doing. Slowly inhale and count to six. Then exhale as you count to six. Keep doing this, extending your inhales and exhales to last for the entire six beats. Focusing on your breath and repeating the simple sequence of numbers will help you calm down.

STRONG GIRL

FINDING STRENGTH IN YOGA

Strength training is a type of exercise that builds up muscle and bone. Even though yoga doesn't involve lifting weights or using fitness machines, it's a great strength training workout. Yoga uses the best strength training tool you have—your own body weight.

Yoga involves isometric strength training. Isometric exercises challenge your muscles to work by holding a weight-bearing position without moving. This means your muscles must stay still in a tensed position. Most yoga classes involve holding different poses for several breaths at a time. At first, the poses might seem simple or even easy. But after a few breaths, the isometric challenge of holding the poses will have you sweating.

Yoga doesn't just strengthen your muscles. It can also strengthen your bones. Over time, our bones can become weaker and more fragile. Activities such as yoga, that encourage safe weight-bearing postures, can help bones stay strong over time.

Almost all types of yoga that involve asanas, or physical poses, can help you increase your strength. One type of yoga is called Ashtanga. It is a vigorous and high-energy practice that involves moving through a series of very challenging poses. Many practitioners of Ashtanga practice up to six times a week.

Stay Safe

Yoga can be a safe, gentle way to build muscle and bone strength if you follow one rule: Never stay in a pose that feels painful. When performed correctly, a yoga pose might make you feel a deep stretch or muscular challenge. But it should never, ever cause pain.

Guru

Pronounced GOO-roo

From the root word *gri* meaning "to praise"

Guru is a Sanskrit word that means teacher, or leader. Many types of yoga were developed by different gurus over time. For example, Ashtanga yoga was developed by a guru named Pattabhi Jois. People all over the world follow his teachings.

TRIANGLE POSE

Sanskrit Name: *Utthita Trikonasana*
Pronunciation: ooh-TEE-tah tree-kon-AHS-ah-nah

Practicing yoga regularly is one of the best ways to maintain a healthy, strong back. Triangle Pose works the muscles in the back while it stretches the neck, legs, shoulders, and feet.

step 1 Stand at the front of your yoga mat. Turn to face the left. Take a big step back with your right foot to bring your feet at least 3 feet (1 meter) apart.

step 2 With straight legs, turn your right toes to point toward the front of your mat. Angle your left foot so that the toes point toward the left front corner of your mat. Point both sides of your hips toward the left side of your mat.

step 3 Extend your arms out to the sides, with palms facing down.

step 4 Pull your shoulder blades closer together. Drop your shoulders away from your ears.

Keep both legs as straight as possible without locking your knees.

step 5 Reach your left fingertips down to rest on your left shin, the floor outside your left foot, or a yoga block.

step 6 Repeat on the other side.

step 7 Hold for several breaths.

Reach your right arm straight up with your palm facing the right side of your mat.

Look straight ahead or challenge yourself by looking up toward your fingers.

Stack your right shoulder over your left shoulder.

63

REVOLVED TRIANGLE

Revolved Triangle takes the stretching and strengthening benefits of triangle pose and adds a challenging twist. It can be tough to balance in this pose, so remember to focus your gaze on something close by.

Sanksrit Name: *Parvrtta Trikonasana*

Pronunciation:

par-VREE-tah tree-kon-AHS-ah-nah

Keep both legs as straight as possible without locking your knees.

step 1   Stand at the front of your yoga mat. Turn to face the right. Take a step back with your right foot to bring your feet about 2.5 feet (0.75 m) apart.

step 2   Slightly bend your left knee and turn your left toes to point toward the front of your mat. Keeping your right leg straight, angle your right foot so that the toes point toward the right front corner of your mat. Press your left heel firmly down into the mat.

step 3   Bring your hands to your hips and square your hips to the front of your yoga mat. To do this, pull your right hip forward and push your left hip back. Point your belly button forward.

step 4   Lift the crown of your head straight up to lengthen your back.

step 5   Bend at the hips to bring your right hand down to the mat just outside your left foot. Keep your left hand on your left hip. If this twist feels too difficult, bring your right hand to the inside of your left foot instead.

step 6   Slowly, begin to straighten your left knee. If this feels too challenging, rest your right fingertips on a block instead of the floor.

step 7   Raise your left arm straight up. Straighten the elbow and face the palm toward the left side of your mat.

step 8   Lift your right ear away from your right shoulder so that your head and neck are in line with your spine. Take three breaths.

step 9   Repeat on the other side.

WARRIOR 3 POSE

Sanskrit Name: *Virabhadrasana 3*

Pronunciation: veer-ah-bah-DRAHS-ah-nah

Warrior 3 Pose can improve your back strength, shoulder flexibility, balance, and focus.

step 1 If you're using a mat, start this pose standing at the back of it. Step your right foot at least 3 feet (1 m) forward. Keep your right toes pointing straight ahead.

step 2 Bend the right knee deeply until it is over the ankle. Lift your arms straight up toward the sky with your palms facing one another.

step 3 Reach your arms forward with straight elbows as you stand on your right foot and extend your left.

Try to keep your torso and leg parallel to the ground.

Keep toes pointed.

step 4 Tilt your torso forward enough that your arms, torso, and lifted left leg form a straight line parallel to the floor.

step 5 Press evenly into all parts of your right foot. Try not to let your weight roll to one side or the other.

step 6 Look directly in front of you or down at your right foot. Hold for a few breaths. Return to high lunge.

step 7 Repeat on other side.

STANDING SPLITS

Sanskrit Name: *Urdhva Prasarita Eka Padasana*

Pronunciation: OOR-dvah prah-sah-REE-ta EH-kah pah-DAS-ah-nah

If you're ready for a real challenge, try mastering the Standing Splits. It's a deep stretch for the standing leg and a great workout for the muscles in your back. Pay attention to which side is easier for you. Most people are more flexible on one side than the other.

step 1 Stand with your feet 4 to 5 inches (10 to 13 cm) apart. Have your toes slightly closer together than your heels.

step 2 Bend at the hips to fold forward. Let both hands dangle toward the floor. If you are able to, rest your fingertips on the mat in front of your feet. If you can't reach the floor, rest your hands on blocks instead.

step 3 Lean your weight into your left foot. Lift your right leg behind you.

An advanced version of this pose adds the challenge of balance. Once you've mastered standing splits with your hands on the floor or on blocks, try it with one or both hands resting on the ankle of the standing leg.

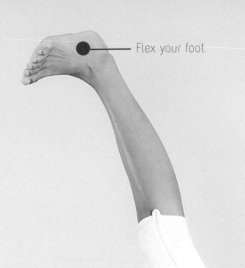

Flex your foot.

step 4 Straighten your right knee as much as possible and flex your foot to point your toes toward the floor. Lift your right heel away from the floor.

step 5 Draw your upper body closer to your left leg as you fold forward even more. Hold for a few breaths.

step 6 Repeat on the other side.

CHAIR POSE

Sanskrit Name: *utkatasana*

Pronounced: oot-kah-TAS-ah-nah

Do you want to strengthen the muscles in your feet, calves, thighs, buns, and back all at once? Try Chair Pose. Who knew taking a seat could be so challenging?

step 1 Place feet 4 to 5 inches (10 to 13 cm) apart, with your toes slightly closer together than your heels.

step 2 Bend the knees deeply, as though you are going to sit down into a chair.

step 3 With straight elbows, raise your arms up. Try to align your upper arms with your ears.

step 4 Rock your weight back into your heels so that your hips are hovering over your heels.

step 5 Draw your upper body closer to your legs as you fold forward even more. Hold for a few breaths.

step 6 Release pose and repeat several times.

Keep your chin
parallel to the floor.

HIGH LUNGE

Few people can agree on the proper Sanskrit name for this pose.
But no one denies that it's a great pose for strengthening your legs.

step 1 From a standing position, take a big step forward with your left leg. Point your left toes straight ahead.

step 2 Bend the left knee deeply while you keep your right leg as straight as you can. Lift your right heel away from the floor so that you are resting on the ball of your right foot.

step 3 Raise both arms up with your palms facing in.

step 4 Try not to allow your shoulders to rise up near your ears. Focus on dropping them down toward the floor. Roll your shoulder blades up and then down toward your bottom.

step 5 Square your hips. To do this, point your hips and belly button toward the front of the room or yoga mat. Hold for several breaths.

step 6 Repeat on the other side.

 Think carefully about your feet in this pose. Press your left big toe down especially hard. Doing this will help you prevent any injuries to your knees while holding this pose.

Face your palms in.

Knee Safety

Keep your knees healthy and safe by always following this rule: Whenever you are bending your knee in a lunging pose, make sure the knee stays above the ankle. If you allow your knee to balance farther forward, above your toes, you might put too much stress on the joint.

Square your hips.

Keep your back leg as straight as you can.

Lift your heel away from the floor.

HORSE POSE

Sanskrit Name: *Utkata Konasana*
Pronounced: OOT-kah-tah kone-AHS-ah-nah

Also known as Goddess Pose, this asana is a good way to gain flexibility in the hips while you strengthen your thighs.

step 1 Take a wide stance, with your heels about 3 feet (1 m) apart. Turn both feet out, so that your toes point out and your heels point in.

step 2 Bend your knees deeply. Try to bring your knees just above your heels.

step 3 Keep your upper body upright. Point your tailbone down and try to balance your shoulders above your hips.

step 4 Bring your palms together in front of your heart. Hold for several breaths.

step 5 Slowly straighten your legs to come out of the pose safely.

 Try not to lean forward in this pose. Imagine you are pressing your back up against a wall.

BRIDGE POSE

Sanskrit Name: *Setu Bandha Sarvangasana*
Pronounced: SET-too BANda sar-vahn-GAS-ah-nah

Try to imagine your body forming the shape of a bridge over a small stream. That's the idea behind the aptly named Bridge Pose.

Press your hands into the mat.

step 1 Lay down on your back.

step 2 Bend your knees and bring your heels close to your bottom. Your feet should be 2 to 3 inches (5 to 8 cm) apart and parallel to one another. Rest your arms down along your sides.

step 3 Press your feet down as you lift your hips up. Keeping your arms at your sides, press them down into your yoga mat. Press the back of your head down into your yoga mat. Try not to let your knees fall out away from each other. They should stay about 3 inches (8 cm) apart during this pose.

step 4 After a few breaths, slowly lie down onto your back again.

Push your legs and torso up.

Resist the urge to pull your knees into your chest after you do this pose. It's tempting, but moving from a back bend to an extreme forward fold can hurt your back.

DOLPHIN POSE

Dolphin Pose is a challenging but safe way to work your arms, shoulders, core, and back. It doesn't have a commonly used Sanskrit name, but it's still part of a balanced yoga practice.

step 1 Start on your hands and knees. From there, drop your forearms to the mat. Make sure your forearms are parallel to one another, and your palms are facing down on the mat.

step 2 With your feet 3 to 4 inches (8 to 10 cm) apart, tuck your toes under. Press into the balls of your feet to lift your knees off of the mat and point your bottom up. If this feels challenging for you, stay in this posture for several breaths and then take a break.

step 3 If you want to try a deeper form of this pose, work on straightening your legs as much as you can by pressing your bottom up toward the sky.

Press your heels toward the ground.

Enter this pose slowly and listen to your body. If you feel any pain, stop immediately.

step 4 Press your chest toward the space between your knees.

step 5 Relax your neck by allowing your head to hang loosely. Your head should not touch the yoga mat.

step 6 Hold for several breaths.

step 7 Bring your knees down to the mat and press back up to your hands to safely come out of this pose.

If full Dolphin Pose is too challenging for you, stop at Step 2. In this slightly easier version, the knees stay bent.

FOREARM PLANK

If you want a quick way to strengthen your arms, shoulders, core, and back, the Forearm Plank is the pose for you. This pose can quickly tire you, so try to hold it for a few breaths. Then take a break before trying it again.

step 1 Start out on your hands and knees. From there, bring your forearms to the mat. Make sure they are parallel to one another and your palms are facing down.

step 2 Stretch both legs out behind you, and tuck your toes. Your heels should rise straight up away from the floor, and the balls of both feet will hold your weight.

step 3 Straighten your legs, and press your tailbone toward your heels. This will help your back stay very straight.

step 4 Pull your shoulders away from your ears and look down between your hands.

step 5 Hold for several breaths, then return to your hands and knees to rest.

Try to keep your back as straight as possible.

If this pose feels too difficult or puts pressure on your lower back, try bringing your knees down to the mat. Keep your bottom low to form a straight line from your knees to your head.

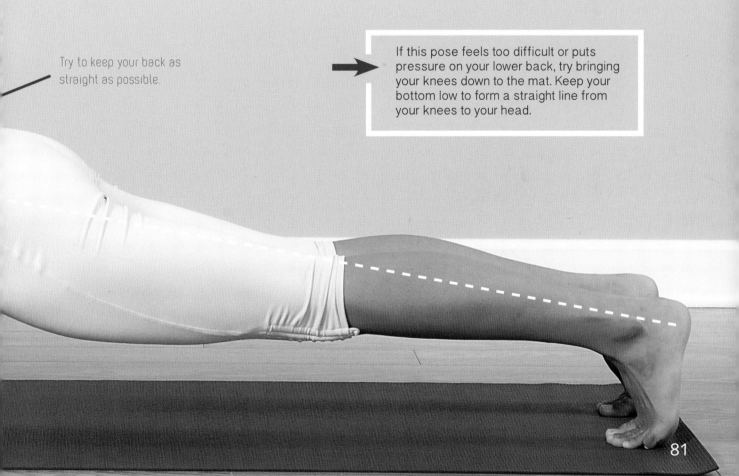

UPWARD FACING PLANK

Sanskrit Name: *Purvottanasana*
Pronounced: purr-voh-ton-AH-sah-nah

Purvottanasana means "intense stretch of the East." While the stretch may be tough, this pose is also an excellent and safe way to strengthen your arms. Make sure to work on finding the correct alignment, or body positioning, in this pose. Safe alignment is the best way to avoid injuries in yoga.

step 1 From a seated position, place your hands a few inches behind your hips with your fingers facing forward. Straighten your arms.

step 2 With bent knees, place your feet on the mat about 1.5 feet (0.5 m) in front of your bottom.

step 3 Lift your bottom off of the mat so that it is at the same height as your knees and shoulders.

Keep your feet as flat as possible.

step 4 One leg at a time, slide your heels forward to straighten each leg. Point your toes so that your feet are as flat on the mat as possible.

step 5 If it feels comfortable, allow your head to drop by relaxing your neck. Hold for a few breaths.

step 6 Carefully lower your bottom down to the mat and rest.

Drop your head back.

Face your fingers forward.

L-POSE

So you think you have this "yoga" thing down? Why not challenge yourself with L-Pose. You might want a friend to help you out when you first try this pose.

Some very advanced yoga students do handstands as part of their practice. L-Pose is also referred to as "half-handstand" because it helps prepare people to work toward doing handstands by building shoulder and back strength.

step 1 Sit against a wall with your bottom pressed against the floorboards and your legs outstretched and straight. Use a towel, water bottle, or other handy item to mark where your heels are on the floor. This way, you know exactly how far one leg-length away from the wall is.

step 2 Come onto your hands and knees with the base of your palms lined up with the marker you used. Place your hands shoulder-distance apart on the floor and point your index fingers straight ahead. Straighten your arms.

step 3 Tuck your toes and place the balls of your feet against the floorboards behind you.

step 4 Slowly start to walk your feet up the wall. Stop when they reach the height of your hips.

Keep your legs parallel to the ground.

step 5 Press your chest toward the wall. Keep your hands flat on the floor and your elbows straight.

step 6 Press your legs as straight as you can. Tighten your stomach muscles, and relax your neck so that your head can hang loosely.

step 7 Hold for a few breaths. Then walk your feet down the wall to rest.

BOW POSE

Sanskrit Name: *Dhanurasana*

Pronounced: don-yur-AH-san-ah

In Bow Pose your body takes the shape of an archer's bow. Not only does this pose give you an intense stretch, but it also strengthens your shoulders at the same time.

step 1   Lie on your belly with your arms down at your sides and your forehead resting on the mat.

step 2   Bend your knees to bring your feet close to your bottom. Reach back and grasp the outer edges of your ankles. Try not to let your knees flop out to the sides when you do this.

Flex your feet

step 2

step 3 Roll your shoulders up and back. Gently lift your head away from your mat and start to kick your heels away from your bottom. This will pull your shoulders farther away from the mat. It will also begin to lift your thighs off the floor.

step 4 Breathe gently and look at something on the floor a few inches in front of your face.

step 5 Slowly release your ankles and straighten your legs out on the mat. Rest your forehead on the mat. Allow your hands to fall comfortably at your sides.

Having trouble grabbing your ankles? Don't worry. Wrap a towel or yoga strap around your ankles and hold onto that instead.

EAGLE POSE

Sanskrit Name: *Garudasana*

Pronounced: gah-roo-dah-AH-san-ah

Eagle Pose combines several challenging elements. Not only does it ask your muscles to hold a tricky position for several breaths, but it also requires you to balance at the same time.

step 1 Stand with your feet 2 to 3 inches (5 to 8 cm) apart. Have your toes slightly closer together than your heels. Let your arms hang at your sides.

step 2 Bend both knees deeply. Lift your left foot off the floor and cross your left knee over your right. If you can, hook your left toes behind your right calf.

step 3 Keeping your legs crossed, bring your arms out to your sides with your palms facing forward.

step 4 Reach your arms forward and cross your left elbow under your right. Bend both elbows to reach your hands up toward the ceiling. If you are able, bring your palms together.

step 5 Keep your knees bent and rock your weight into your right heel. Lift your elbows so that they are at the same height as your shoulders. Look straight ahead. Hold for a few breaths.

step 6 Slowly uncross your legs and arms, and stand on both feet. Repeat this pose on the other side.

Your sight plays a big role in finding balance. Try this experiment: Do Eagle Pose while looking at a steady object a few feet in front of you. Try Eagle Pose again with your eyes closed. Which version was more challenging for you?

EXTENDED SIDE ANGLE POSE

Sanskrit Name: *Utthita Parsvakonasana*
Pronounced: OOH-teet-ah pars-voh-koe-NAH-san-ah

Extended Side Angle Pose works your shoulders as well as your legs, core, and back. This pose will strengthen your whole body.

step 1   From a standing position, take a big step forward with your left leg. Point your left toes straight ahead.

step 2   Bend the left knee deeply while you keep your right leg as straight as you can. Turn your right heel down so that your whole foot is touching the mat.

! For the most advanced version of this pose, place your left hand outside your left foot for a deep side stretch.

Try to form a straight line from your toes to your fingertips.

step 3 Bring your left elbow to your left thigh. If this feels challenging, stay here. If you want more of a stretch, bring your left fingertips to the mat outside of your left foot.

step 4 Reach your right arm up. Open your chest to the right side of your mat. Then slowly reach your right arm forward until it is in the same line as your right leg. Turn your palm down toward the floor. Hold for a few breaths.

step 5 Repeat on the other side.

BOAT POSE

Sanskrit Name: *Navasana*
Pronounced: nah-VAS-ah-nah

The core muscles are those that surround your hips, belly, and low back. Almost all yoga poses work the muscles in your core. However, some poses challenge these muscles more than others. Boat Pose is a wonderful core exercise.

step 1 Sit on your mat with your legs outstretched in front of you. Reach your arms forward, with your palms facing in.

step 2 Slowly lean back until your legs feel very heavy. Then bend your knees up toward the sky until you are resting on your heels and bottom. Keep reaching your arms forward.

Keep your chin up.

Arms should be parallel with legs

Keep your back as straight as possible.

step 3
With your knees bent, lift your heels off the ground. If this feels difficult, remain in this position. If you want more of a challenge, raise your heels until your shins are parallel to the floor.

step 4
Hold for a few breaths.

step 5
Slowly lower your heels to the mat and return to a seated position to rest.

Yogi and Yogini
Pronounced: YO-gee and yoh-GEE-nee

From the root *Yuj* meaning "one who is joined or connected"

You might hear yoga teachers referring to *yogis* and *yoginis*. Who are they talking about? *Yogi* is the term used to describe male yoga students. *Yogini* is the term for female yoga students.

! For the most advanced version of this pose, straighten your legs. Your body will form the shape of a V.

Straighten your legs as much as you can.

BIRD DOG POSE

When you are doing Bird Dog Pose, you might not feel your core muscles working, but they are. This seemingly simple pose works the muscles in your abdomen, lower back, upper back, and legs.

step 1 Start on your hands and knees. Have your knees the same width as your hips, and have your hands directly beneath your shoulders.

step 2 Firm the muscles of your belly by pulling your belly button in toward your spine.

step 3 Extend your left arm forward with your palm facing in. Straighten your elbow.

Flex your top foot.

Tuck your bottom toes under.

step 4 Tuck your left toes under. Then extend your right leg straight behind you. Your right toes should point straight down. Straighten your knee as much as you can.

step 5 Do not allow your belly to fall down toward the mat. If you feel this happening, keep pulling your belly button in toward your spine.

step 6 Look straight down at your yoga mat. Hold for a few breaths.

step 7 Repeat on the other side.

Face your palm in.

Look straight down.

SIDE PLANK

Sanskrit Name: *Vasisthasana*

Pronounced: vash-eesh-TAS-ah-nah

Side Plank is a fun variation on Plank Pose. The full version of this pose challenges you to use only one hand and the edge of one foot to balance. If this feels too difficult, don't be afraid to modify the pose.

step 1 Start out in full Plank Pose with knees lifted away from the floor.

Form one straight line with your arms and another from your head to your toes.

step 2 Roll your weight onto the outer edge of your right foot, and stack your left foot on top of your right. At the same time, lift your left arm straight up into the air with the palm facing forward.

step 3   Press your hips upward so that your body forms a straight line from the crown of your head down through your heels. Hold for a few breaths.

step 4   Return to plank pose by dropping the lifted hand and foot to the mat.

step 5   Bend your knees to rest on your hands and knees.

step 6   Repeat on the other side.

For a slightly easier version of the pose, try bending your right knee and stepping your right foot directly in front of the left knee.

GARLAND POSE

Sanskrit Name: *Malasana*
Pronounced: mal-AHS-an-ah

Are you ready to strengthen your feet?
That's right—your feet. This simple
squat stretches your hips and thighs while
strengthening your back and feet.

step 1   Stand with your feet about 4 to 5 inches (10 to 13 cm) apart. Turn your toes out to the side.

step 2   Bend your knees to come into a deep squatting position. Allow your knees to open up to the sides.

step 3   Try to keep your heels on the ground. If this feels like too deep of a stretch, take your feet farther apart and try again.

step 4   Bring your palms together in front of your heart. Press your elbows against the inside edges of both knees.

step 5   Straighten your back as much as you can. Lift your chin slightly away from your chest. Hold for a few breaths.

A simple way to modify this pose is to roll up a towel or yoga blanket and place it under your heels. This will make the stretch less intense in your feet.

EXTENDED HAND-TO-TOE POSE

Sanskrit Name: *Utthita Hasta Padangustasana*
Pronounced: ooh-TEE-tah HAH-sta pah-dahn-goo-STAS-ah-nah

Many yoga poses use binds. Binds are arm positions in which the hands clasp one another, or grasp a body part. Binds work the muscles in the hands. Extended Hand-to-Toe Pose is a nice way to strengthen your hands and feet and work on balance at the same time.

step 1 Stand with your feet 4 to 5 inches (10 to 13 cm) apart. Have your toes slightly closer together than your heels. Bring your right hand to your right hip.

step 2 Lean your weight into your right leg. Lift your left foot off the ground and bring your left knee up in front of your hip.

step 3 Grasp your left big toe with the index and middle fingers of your left hand. Slowly extend your left leg out in front of you as much as you can. Don't worry if your leg doesn't become completely straight.

step 4 Keeping your gaze locked on something in front of you, slowly bring your left leg out to the left. Keep your hips facing forward.

If this stretch feels too intense, modify this pose. Instead of grasping the left toes, hold on to the outer edge of your left knee. Keep your knee bent and back straight as you open your left leg out to the left.

Keep your leg as straight as possible

step 5 Hold for a few breaths.

step 6 Repeat on the other side.

DANCER POSE

Sanskrit Name: *Natarajasana*
Pronounced: nah-tar-ah-JAS-ah-nah

Dancer Pose challenges your balance, flexibility, and the muscles in your hands—all at the same time. Try this pose holding a wall or chair if you find it difficult to balance.

step 1 Stand with your feet 4 to 5 inches (10 to 13 cm) apart. Have your toes slightly closer together than your heels. Reach your left arm straight up into the sky.

step 2 Lean your weight into your right leg. Kick your left foot toward your bottom, and grasp the outer edge of your left foot with your left hand.

step 3 Point your left knee straight down toward the floor. Try to keep your left knee from opening out to the left.

step 4 Slowly start to press your left foot into your left hand. Your heel will come away from your bottom as you start to stretch.

step 5 Carefully begin to lean your upper body forward and reach your right arm straight out in front of you, palm facing down. Hold for a few breaths.

step 6 Slowly and carefully lift your upper body to an upright position and release your lifted left foot to the floor.

step 7 Repeat on the other side.

Clasp the outside of your foot.

If it's difficult to grab your left foot with your left hand, hold a towel or yoga strap wrapped around your ankle instead.

FIT GIRL

Is Yoga Just for FLEXIBLE People?

You're no couch potato. But you get tired of doing the same old workout routine. You can only jog around the block so many times before boredom creeps in. It's time to mix things up, and yoga might just be the answer.

Go ahead—flex your muscles. Want to see more definition? One of the biggest perks of a regular yoga practice is that it builds muscle. Practice yoga regularly and you'll see muscles you didn't even know you had! Not only does yoga help you grow stronger, but it also helps you become more flexible. This is an important counterpart to having muscular strength. After all, what good are toned hamstrings if you can't reach down to tie your shoes?

Yoga is a combination of three things: physical poses called asanas, controlled breathing called pranayama, and meditation. When used together, this combo benefits people of all ages. In fact, people who practice yoga often report that they sleep better, get sick less often, feel happier, and are less overwhelmed by worries.

When is the last time you touched your toes? If it's been a while, don't worry. One myth about yoga is that only flexible people can do it. But practicing yoga on a regular basis is actually one of the best ways to *become* flexible. Yoga poses can be modified for any yoga student, regardless of how flexible he or she is.

Vinyasa yoga is one type of yoga that can help people become more flexible. This type of yoga involves flowing from pose to pose. There is less rest between poses, which can make this type of yoga physically challenging.

Pranayama

Pronounced: prah-nah-YAH-mah

From the root *prana* meaning "breath" or "life force"

Pranayama is the practice of controlling the breath. It often involves retaining, or holding the breath for a few seconds at a time in a careful rhythm directed by an instructor.

SUN SALUTATION A

Sanskrit Name: *Surya Namaskar A*
Pronounced: SIR-yah NAH-ma-skar AYE

Almost all yoga classes will include Sun Salutations. Sun Salutations are a sequence of poses designed to energize the body, warm the muscles, and help people get focused on their body. Sun Salutations involve large gentle movements. They increase blood flow to all the muscle groups of the body. In a typical yoga practice, you will do at least three Sun Salutations at the start of class. Then you might continue to do Sun Salutations between poses to raise your heart rate or keep your muscles warm.

Sun Salutations have ancient roots. The name *namaskar* comes from the word *nama*, which means to "bow down" or "adore." When early yoga students practiced Sun Salutations, they were bowing down to the sun. Today people still value the symbolism of this activity. It's a reminder of the importance of the sun to the living things that need it.

MOUNTAIN POSE

Sanskrit Name: *Tadasana*
Pronounced: Tah-DAH-sah-nah

step 1 Mountain Pose starts out each Sun Salutation. To begin, stand at the top of your mat, with your big toes touching and your heels slightly separated.

step 2 Spread your toes out on the mat.

step 3 Stand up tall. Roll your shoulders down your back. Bring your shoulder blades closer together and pull them down.

step 4 Let your arms hang at your sides. Face your palms forward.

step 5 Lift your chin slightly so that your jawbone is parallel to the floor.

Drop your shoulders and lengthen your neck.

Face your palms forward.

FORWARD FOLD

Sanskrit Name: *Uttanasana*
Pronounced: ooh-tah-NAH-sah-nah

After Mountain Pose, the Sun Salutation moves into a Forward Fold. This might seem like a simple movement, but it's actually a challenge to focus on finding the right alignment. Paying attention to the position of your feet, back, knees, and gaze will make this seemingly easy pose very challenging.

step 1 Start in Mountain Pose. Inhale and lift your arms up.

step 2 With a slight bend in your knees, exhale and bend at the hips to fold forward.

step 3 Allow your hands to rest on your shins, ankles, the floor, or on blocks.

step 4 If this feels challenging, keep your knees slightly bent. If you want more of a stretch, slowly straighten your knees.

HALF-FORWARD FOLD

Sanskrit Name: *Arda Uttanasana*

Pronounced: ARE-duh ooh-tah-NAH-sah-nah

step 1 From Forward Fold, you will move into the next pose in the Sun Salutation. Inhale and lift your head and shoulders away from the floor.

step 2 With straight elbows, rest your hands on the floor, blocks, your ankles, or your shins.

step 3 Extend the crown of your head forward, so that your back becomes straight.

step 4 Focus your gaze on the mat.

step 5 Return to your full Forward Fold as you exhale.

FOUR-LIMBED STAFF POSE

Sanskrit Name: *Chaturanga Dandasana*

Pronounced: chah-turr-AN-gah don-DAHS-ah-nah

After your Forward Fold, you will move into Four-Limbed Staff Pose. This pose takes a bit of practice to get down. Asking a friend to watch you move through this pose can be very helpful. She can let you know if you need to adjust your alignment.

step 1 From your Forward Fold, bend your knees enough to bring both palms flat on your yoga mat just outside of your feet. Your hands should be about shoulder-distance apart on the mat.

step 2 Step back into Plank Pose. This pose looks like you are about to do a pushup. Have your feet about 2 to 3 inches (5 to 8 cm) apart, and rest your weight on the balls of your feet. Make sure your shoulders are right above your wrists.

Plank Pose

step 3 Straighten your back as much as possible. A good way to do this is to point your tailbone toward your heels. At the same time, point the crown of your head forward.

step 4 Bend your elbows to lower your body halfway down to the mat. Stop when your elbows are at the same height as your shoulders. Make sure to keep your elbows tucked in close to your ribcage. Do not let them bend out to the sides the way you might in a typical pushup.

If this feels too challenging or hurts your back in any way, modify this pose by bringing your knees to the mat. It is better to modify a move and keep proper form than to push your body to do things it's not ready for.

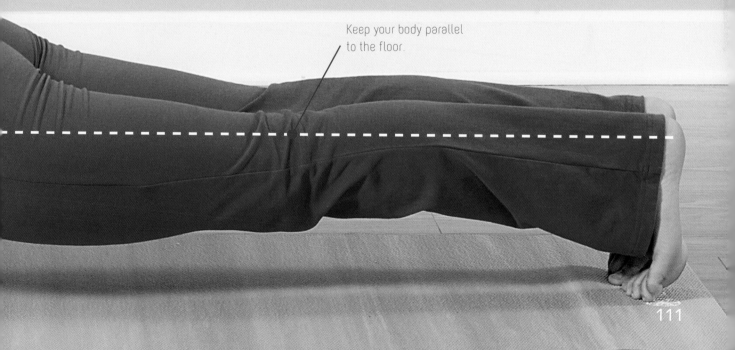

Keep your body parallel to the floor.

Four-Limbed Staff Pose is typically followed by one of two back-bending poses: Cobra Pose or Upward Facing Dog Pose. Cobra is a gentler pose. If you tweaked your back carrying too many books, this is the pose for you. If you're looking for more of a challenge to your core, shoulders, and legs, give Upward Facing Dog a try.

COBRA POSE

Sanskrit Name: *Bhujangasana*
Pronounced: boo-john-GAHS-ah-nah

step 1 From Four-Limbed Staff Pose, lower your stomach down to your mat.

step 2 Point your toes and press the tops of your feet into the mat.

step 3 Roll your shoulders up and back. Then press into your hands to lift your head and shoulders away from the mat. Lift your chin slightly.

step 4 Keep your elbows slightly bent and pinned to your sides. Try to use the muscles in your back and the muscles in your arms to hold this gentle backbend.

UPWARD FACING DOG

Sanskrit Name: *Urdhva Mukha Svanasana*
Pronounced: OORD-vah MOOK-ah svan-AHS-ah-nah

step 1 From Four-Limbed Staff Pose you could move right into Upward Facing Dog instead of Cobra pose. Just press your weight into the tops of the feet and lift the rest of your body up. Keep your knees straight.

step 2 Straighten your elbows to lift your shoulders away from the floor. At the same time, drop your hips to come into a backbend. Keep your knees and hips off the mat.

step 3 Pull your shoulders down away from your ears and lift your chin slightly.

DOWNWARD FACING DOG

Sanskrit Name: *Adho Mukha Svanasana*

Pronounced: AH-doh MOOK-ah svan-AHS-ah-nah

You'll finish your Sun Salutation in yoga's most famous pose—Downward Facing Dog. In many yoga classes, you will do this pose over and over again. Because it is such a staple of most yoga practices, it's important to do it correctly.

step 1 From Cobra Pose or Upward Facing Dog Pose, tuck your toes under and use the muscles of your core to lift your bottom up. Your body will form the shape of an upside down V.

step 2 Press your heels toward the mat. If you are able, straighten your knees. If this feels too intense, allow your knees to stay bent.

Press down through all parts of your palms.

step 3 Press all parts of your hands evenly down into the mat, especially the area around your thumb and the base of each finger. Don't let all of your weight rest on your wrists. This can lead to painful joint problems.

step 4 Pull your belly in toward your spine.

Try to think about your Sun Salutations as a way to rev up your yoga practice. Add a Sun Salutation in at any point during your yoga practice. Doing this will energize your body and refocus your mind.

Pull your belly button in toward your spine.

Press your heels down toward the mat.

Using YOGA to Gain
FLEX-IBLITY

After a few Sun Salutations, you're probably feeling the burn. The time is right to work on poses that build flexibility. Yoga is a safe way to become more flexible because it lengthens your muscles without overstretching or injuring them. Yoga requires you to keep your muscles active as you stretch. When muscles are completely relaxed, they can be easily injured.

Don't hurry to become more flexible. A regular yoga practice will help you to gradually build flexibility over time. It can be tempting to try to push yourself to achieve different challenging poses you see other people doing. But it's much safer to pace yourself. Slow and steady is the way to go.

→ Don't lock your joints while practicing yoga. Always keep a very slight bend in joints such as your knees and elbows. Doing this will keep your muscles active. It will also prevent you from overstretching.

WARRIOR 1 POSE

Sanskrit Name: *Virabhadrasana*
Pronounced: vee-rah-bah-DRAS-ah-nah

It might seem odd to hear a yoga pose called "warrior." After all, we often think of yoga as a peaceful activity. This pose is named in honor of a special type of warrior—the spiritual warrior. Traditionally, the people who practiced yoga in ancient India were fighting to learn more about themselves. Because of this, they are sometimes called warriors of the spirit.

step 1 From Downward Facing Dog, step your left foot forward between your hands.

step 2 Turn your right heel down to the mat. The inner edge of your right foot should press down into the mat. Keep your right leg straight.

step 3 Inhale and lift your upper body and arms up. Straighten your elbows and face your palms toward one another. Relax your shoulders down away from your ears.

step 4 Exhale and bend deeply into your left knee until it hovers over your left ankle.

step 5 Lift your chin and look up between your hands. Hold for a few breaths.

step 6 Return to Downward Facing Dog Pose. Repeat on the other side.

Press your heel
into the mat.

HALF-SPLITS POSE

Sanskrit Name: *Ardha Hanumanasana*
Pronounced: ARE-duh hah-noo-mah-NAHS-ah-nah

Half-Splits Pose is also sometimes called Half-Monkey God Pose. This name comes from a story about Hanuman, a god from the Hindu religion. In the story, Hanuman leaps across an ocean with one leg stretched out in front of him and one stretched behind him. When people do the full version of the pose, they resemble Hanuman as he leapt.

step 1 From Downward Facing Dog, step your right foot forward between your hands. Bend your right knee deeply.

step 2 Bring your left knee down to the mat. Keep your left toes tucked under and your left heel lifted.

step 3 Bring your hands to either side of your right knee on the mat.

120

step 4 Slowly start to straighten your right knee by moving your hips backward. Stop when the stretch feels challenging but not painful.

step 5 Try to hover your hips above your left knee. If you need to, move your left knee back on the mat a few inches.

step 6 Flex your right foot so that your toes point straight up.

step 7 Fold your head and chest forward.

! The full version of this pose is very challenging. Work with a yoga instructor to make sure you have the correct alignment.

Splits Pose

Tuck your toes under.

WIDE-LEGGED FORWARD FOLD

Sanskrit Name: *Prasarita Padottanasana*

Pronounced: prah-sah-REE-tah pah-doh-tah-NAHS-ah-nah

The Wide-Legged Forward Fold provides a challenging stretch in what looks like an easy pose. But if your muscles are engaged and properly aligned, your back, thighs, and feet will all be working hard.

step 1   Start in Mountain Pose.

step 2   Take a big step out to the right so that your feet are at least 3 feet (1 meter) apart. Have your toes slightly closer together than your heels.

step 3   Bring your hands to your hips.

step 4   Put a slight bend in your knees and bend at the hips to fold forward.

step 5   Bring your hands down to the mat directly under your shoulders.

step 6   As you inhale, straighten your elbows and lift your upper body halfway away from the floor.

Mountain Pose

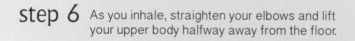

step 7 As you exhale, bend your elbows and fold forward. Keep the muscles in your back active by pulling your shoulder blades toward your hips.

step 8 Press evenly into the inner and outer edges of your feet.

step 9 If you are able, slowly begin to straighten your knees but stop before you lock them.

123

COW-FACE POSE

Sanskrit Name: *Gomukhasana*
Pronounced: go-moo-KAHS-ah-nah

If you look closely at Cow-Face Pose, you might be able to see how it resembles a cow's face. The crossed legs look like a cow's crooked jaw. The elbows look like a cow's floppy ears. This oddly named pose works your back and core while stretching your hips and shoulders.

step 1 Start on your hands and knees. Cross your left knee behind your right. Allow your feet to fall out to the sides.

step 2 Slowly, walk your hands back as you sit your bottom down between your heels. If this feels like too much of a stretch on your knees, place a block between your ankles and sit on that.

step 3 Bring your upper body upright to sit up tall.

step 4   Lift your left arm straight up. Bend the left elbow to reach your hand toward your middle back.

step 5   Reach your right arm straight out to the right with your palm facing behind you. Bend your right elbow to bring the back of your right hand toward the middle of your back.

step 6   If you are able, clasp your hands behind your back. If this is too challenging, either hold a yoga strap or towel between your hands, or simply grab hold of your shirt with each hand.

step 7   Lift your chin slightly and sit up straight. Hold for a few breaths.

step 8   Repeat on the other side.

COBBLER'S POSE

Sanskrit Name: *Baddha Konasana*
Pronounced: BAH-dah kone-AHS-ah-nah

Do you need an excuse to inspect your pedicure? Cobbler's Pose will give you that chance. Cobblers are people who repair shoes. Cobbler's Pose looks like someone examining the soles of her shoes. This pose stretches your hips, low back, and neck.

step 1 Start sitting on your mat. Bring the soles of your feet together, and let your knees fall open to the sides.

step 2 Slide your feet closer to your body until you begin to feel a stretch in your hips. This will be a different distance for everyone. Some people might be able to bring their heels all the way to the body, while others might have to stop when their heels are 12 or 18 inches (30 or 45 cm) away. Either way is okay.

step 3 Sit up tall. Pull your shoulders down away from your ears.

step 4 Bring your thumbs to the balls of your feet and pull the big toe sides of your feet open. It will look a little like you are opening a book.

step 5 Keep your hips relaxed. Pull your belly button in toward your spine. Hold for a few breaths.

Alignment matters in this pose. If your knees begin to rise up higher than your hips, sit on top of a yoga block. This way you can keep your knees at the same height as your hips.

127

ONE-LEGGED KING PIGEON POSE

Sanskrit Name: *Eka Pada Rajakapotasana*

Pronounced: EH-kah PAH-dah rah-jah-cop-poh-TAHS-ah-nah

If you thought Cow-Face Pose was an odd name, One-Legged King Pigeon Pose may seem even stranger. Whether you say the English or Sanskrit name for this pose, your tongue is going to get as much of a workout as the rest of your body. One-Legged King Pigeon Pose stretches the hips, an area of the body that most people find very tight.

step 1 Start in Downward Facing Dog Pose. Lift your left foot away from the mat.

step 2 Bring your left foot forward to rest on the mat behind your right hand. At the same time, rest your left knee behind your left hand. The outside of your left shin will rest against the floor. If you are very flexible, your left shin might be parallel to the top of your mat. However, for most people, it will be on an angle.

Downward Facing Dog

Point your toes

step 3 Point your right toes. Allow your right knee to rest on the mat.

step 4 Let your hips fall toward the mat. If this feels painful, place a block or blanket under the left side of your bottom and rest your weight on it. Otherwise, allow your bottom to rest on the mat.

step 5 Keep your upper body upright. Look straight ahead.

step 6 Hold for a few breaths. Carefully return to Downward Facing Dog.

step 7 Repeat on the other side.

STANDING PIGEON POSE

If you'd like to focus on balance in addition to stretching, try Standing Pigeon Pose. It offers a deep stretch without putting as much pressure on your hips as One-Legged King Pigeon. Don't be fooled, though—this variation isn't necessarily easier.

step 1 Start in Mountain Pose.

step 2 Bend both knees deeply, as if you were about to sit into a chair.

step 3 Keeping your left knee bent, bring your right ankle on top of the left knee.

step 4 Bring your palms together in front of your heart.

step 5 Bend your left knee more deeply to sit even lower. Keep your right foot flexed.

step 6 Relax your shoulders. Pull your belly button in toward your spine and keep your upper body tall. Focus your gaze on something directly in front of you.

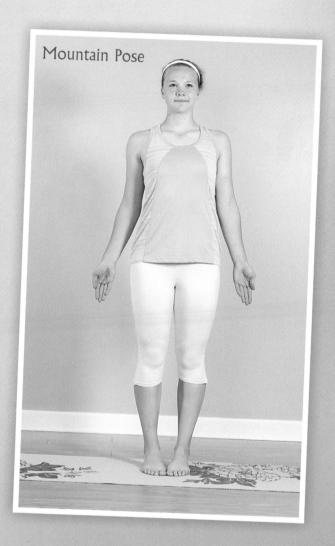

Mountain Pose

Press your hands together over your heart.

step 7 Hold for a few breaths. Slowly return to Mountain Pose.

step 8 Repeat on the other side.

Flex your foot.

UPWARD-FACING BOW POSE

Sanskrit Name: *Urdhva Dhanurasana*

Pronounced: OOR-dva don-your-AHS-ah-nah

Do you ever feel like you're bending over backward to get everything done in your busy schedule? Upward-Facing Bow Pose will teach you to do just that—literally! This pose is an intense, invigorating backbend. With careful practice almost anyone can enjoy this pose.

step 1   Lie on your back on your yoga mat.

step 2   Bend your knees up, and set your feet on the mat a few inches in front of your bottom. Have your feet no wider than the width of your hips.

step 3   Bring your hands with the palms down onto the mat beside your ears with your thumbs pointing toward your cheeks. Have your hands about shoulder-distance apart on the mat. If you have them too close together, this pose can be difficult. Your elbows should rise straight up. Do not allow them to fall out to the sides.

step 3

step 4 As you inhale, press your feet down to lift your hips off the mat. Press into the inner edges of both feet to keep your knees from falling out to the sides.

step 5 As you exhale, press into your hands to lift your head off the mat. Look to the back of your mat to bring the crown of your head down onto the mat.

step 6 Gently pause on the crown of your head without putting pressure on your neck. Bring your elbows slightly closer together, and pull your shoulder blades closer together on your back.

step 7 Pause for a few breaths on the crown of your head. Keep pressing down into the mat with your hands so that you aren't supporting much weight with your head.

step 8 If this feels like a good challenge, stay here. Hold this pose for a few breaths. Then slowly lower to your back for a rest. If you'd like to push yourself even more, turn the page.

UPWARD-FACING BOW POSE
continued

step 9 If you want to try the full Upward-Facing Bow Pose, press into your hands and straighten your elbows to lift your head off the mat.

step 10 Try your best to bring your shoulders directly over your wrists.

step 11 Keep pressing into the inner edges of your feet as you lift your hips higher to bring your knees directly over your ankles. Hold for a few breaths.

step 12 To come out of this pose, tuck your chin into your chest.

step 13 Slowly bend your elbows to return to your back.

step 14 Remain on your back for a few breaths to rest.

step 15 One leg at a time, straighten your knees to lie flat on your mat.

It can be helpful to ask a friend to watch you do this pose to check your alignment.

PYRAMID POSE

Sanskrit Name: *Parsvottanasana*

Pronounced: pars-voh-toe-NAS-ah-nah

Pyramid Pose combines a deep forward fold with an intense hip and thigh stretch. It is also a challenge to balance. Try to think about your alignment as much as possible in this pose. It's better to be in proper alignment and not stretch as deeply. If you force yourself into the full stretch without the right alignment you could risk injury.

step 1   Start in Downward Facing Dog Pose.

Downward Facing Dog

Straighten your front leg as much as is comfortable.

step 2 Step both feet forward about 12 inches (30 cm).

step 3 Look forward, and step your right foot up between your hands.

step 4 Turn your left heel down and press the inner edge of your left foot down into the mat. Keep your left leg straight.

step 5 Bring your fingertips to the mat on either side of your right foot, or allow them to rest on blocks.

step 6 Slowly begin to straighten your right knee. Stop before the stretch becomes painful.

step 7 Allow your upper body to fold forward over your right leg.

step 8 Square your hips. Hold for several breaths.

step 9 Return to Downward Facing Dog Pose. Repeat on the other side.

Keep your back leg straight.

BIG TOE POSE

Sanskrit Name: *Padangusthasana*

Pronounced: pah-dahn-goose-TAHS-ah-nah

You probably never thought something called Big Toe Pose could provide a deep stretch for the shoulders and neck. But think again! Big Toe Pose uses a simple bind to incorporate the upper body in an easy way. Binds can make a pose more intense.

step 1 Start in Mountain Pose. Reach your arms up.

step 2 With a slight bend in your knees, bend at the hips to fold forward. Allow your hands to fall down toward the mat.

step 3 Bend your knees as much as you need to in order to reach your toes. Hold onto your big toes with your first two fingers. Do not rest your thumbs on the mat.

step 4 As you inhale, slightly lift your head and chest away from the floor. Straighten your elbows and lengthen your back as much as possible. Do not let go of your toes.

step 5 Exhale and fold forward. If you can, start to straighten your knees very slowly.

Mountain Pose

step 6 If you are able to straighten your knees, bend your elbows out to the sides. Pull your upper body closer to your thighs.

step 7 Hold for a few breaths. Return to Mountain Pose.

LOW-LUNGE POSE

Sanskrit Name: *Anjanayasana*

Pronounced: on-jen-eh-AHS-ah-nah

It's time to get low! Low-Lunge Pose stretches your hips, thighs, and ankles while strengthening your upper back and arms.

step 1 From Downward Facing Dog Pose, step your right foot forward between your hands.

step 2 Drop your left knee to the mat, and point your left toes.

step 3 Bring both hands to the top of your right knee.

step 4 Slowly begin to move your hips forward until you feel a deep stretch in the front of your left hip and right buttock.

step 5 Inhale and lift your arms up with your palms facing one another. Straighten your elbows.

Keep your toes flat on the floor

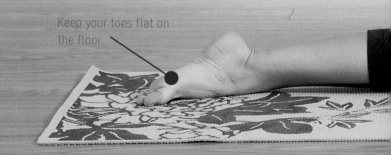

step 6 Lift your gaze slightly to bring your chin parallel to the floor. Hold for a few breaths.

step 7 Return to Downward Facing Dog. Repeat on the other side.

Keep your knee above your ankle

TWISTED LOW-LUNGE POSE

Are you ready for a move with a twist? Twisting poses tighten up your core and the muscles of your back. If you have a yoga block and strap, keep them handy. You can use one or both props to modify this move.

Low-Lunge Pose

step 1 Start in Low-Lunge Pose with your right foot forward.

step 2 Put your left hand on the mat while you bring your right hand to the top of your right knee. Press into your right hand to turn your chest open to the right. Take a few deep breaths. If this feels challenging, stay here.

step 3 If you want more of a stretch, bend your left knee to bring your heel close to your bottom. Reach back with your right hand to take the outside of your left ankle.

step 4 Gently kick your left foot away from your bottom to engage the muscles in your left leg. Hold for a few breaths.

step 5 Return to Downward Facing Dog Pose. Repeat on the other side.

Downward
Facing Dog

143

TWISTED LOW-LUNGE POSE
modifications

Twisted Low-Lunge Pose can offer intense stretches. If they're too intense for you, a couple easy modifications can help. Put a yoga block under your left hand, and use a yoga strap to extend your reach. Whether you use one or both of these modifications, it's important to keep your form and alignment in mind.

If you find yourself losing your balance in this pose, a yoga block can offer extra stability.

If you can't comfortably bend your knee to the point that your arm can grasp your foot, use a yoga strap. The strap will extend your reach. Using both props still gives you a beneficial pose for building strength and flexibility.

WIDE LOW-LUNGE POSE

The Wide Low-Lunge Pose provides a deep stretch for the hips, thighs, and lower back. It may not have a Sanskrit name, but with a stretch like that, it's quite a popular yoga pose.

step 1 Start in Downward Facing Dog Pose. Step your right foot to the outside of your right hand. Make sure your left toes point straight forward.

step 2 Keep your left knee lifted as you slowly lower your hips to bring your shoulders over your wrists. Keep your right knee hugging into your right shoulder. If this feels challenging, stay here for a few breaths.

step 2

If the stretch in the hip and buttock is too intense for you in this pose, bring your left knee down to the mat.

step 3 If you are interested in a more intense stretch, one at a time, slowly lower to your forearms. Bring your elbows just under your shoulders on the mat. Keep your left leg as straight as possible. Keep your right knee close to your right shoulder. Hold for a few breaths.

step 4 Return to Downward Facing Dog Pose. Repeat on the other side.

TWISTED EXTENDED HAND-TO-TOE POSE

Sanskrit Name: *Utthita Hasta Padangusthasana*

Pronounced: ooh-TEE-tah HAH-sta pah-dahn-goo-STAS-ah-nah

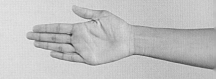

This twisting version of Hand-to-Big-Toe Pose stretches the muscles in your legs and shoulders while it works the muscles of your core, back, and arms. It can be very challenging, so check out the tips to modify it if you need to.

Mountain Pose

step 1 Start in Mountain Pose.

step 2 Lift your right foot off the ground by bringing the knee straight up into the air.

step 3 Take your left hand to the outside of the right foot. Rest your right hand on your right hip.

step 4 Stand tall by lifting your chin and straightening your back as much as you can. Slowly begin to straighten the right leg by pressing your foot forward. Your leg does not have to become completely straight, so stop straightening the knee when this stretch begins to feel intense.

step 5 Extend your right arm out behind you. Open your chest to the right.

step 6 Either look straight ahead, or challenge yourself by looking back over your right thumb.

step 7 Hold for a few breaths. Return to Mountain Pose.

step 8 Repeat on the other side.

There are two easy ways to modify this pose:

1. If it's hard to reach your foot, try holding on to the outside of the knee instead. Do not extend the leg if you are holding the knee. Simply work on twisting open to the side instead.

2. If you can reach your foot, but have difficulty straightening the leg, try wrapping a yoga strap around the foot to extend your reach. Then follow the rest of the directions for this pose.

1.

2.

BROKEN TOE POSE

You might think a lot about your shoes, but what about your feet? This pose stretches the tight muscles along the bottoms of your feet. It might feel intense, so start small. Try holding this pose for just a few breaths to start. Then work up to 30 seconds or even a minute.

step 1 Come to your hands and knees. Bring your knees and feet together so that they touch.

step 2 Tuck your toes under and sit back onto your heels. Allow your hands to rest on your thighs with your palms facing down.

step 3 Bring your upper body upright by lifting the crown of your head straight up. Lift your chin slightly so that it is parallel to the floor. Relax the muscles in your jaw.

step 4 Close your eyes. Take a few deep breaths.

step 5 Lift your hips off of your heels and point your toes. Sit back onto your feet to rest.

This pose can feel very intense, but remember to stop what you're doing if you feel any pain.

Keep your back straight.

Tuck your toes under.

151

HERO POSE

Sanskrit Name: *Virasana*
Pronounced: veer-AHS-ah-nah

That's right, girl. Be a hero! Hero Pose stretches the muscles in the tops of the feet and thighs, while also strengthening the low back. Because this pose allows you to sit fairly still, it can be a nice time to focus your thoughts on your breathing. When you begin working on this pose, you might only hold it for a few breaths. Over time, you may be able to sit in this pose for five minutes or more.

step 1 From your hands and knees, separate your feet so that they are slightly wider than your hips. Press the tops of your feet down into the mat.

step 2 Walk your hands back toward the outsides of your hips as you slowly sit between your heels.

step 3 Sit up tall by lifting the crown of your head straight up. Lift your chin slightly until it is parallel to the floor.

step 4 Draw your shoulder blades down. Pull your belly in.

step 5 Return to hands and knees to rest.

If sitting between your ankles feels too intense or hurts your knees at all, try this modification: Place a block between your ankles and sit on it. You'll still get the great stretch and benefits of Hero Pose, but you won't hurt your knees.

SMART GIRL

Using Yoga to Boost Your
BRAIN POWER

You're already pretty smart. Want to boost your G.P.A. even more? Instead of heading to the library to study, you might want to try yoga. That's right, put down your calculator and drop your dictionary. Grab a bottle of water and get started. Practicing yoga is a fun and easy way to build some mental muscle.

Yoga usually involves three elements—yoga poses, meditation, and controlled breathing. Doing yoga poses works your brain because it forces you to concentrate on your alignment in each pose. Meditation also helps your brain. Meditation is the practice of focusing the mind on one thought or idea for several minutes at a time. Controlled breathing in yoga is often called pranayama. It requires you to think carefully about every breath you take. Combined, these elements can create the ultimate workout for your brain. Even practicing yoga for just 20 minutes can help you improve your focus, learn new things, and think more clearly.

Some yoga poses are especially beneficial for your brain. Poses that stretch and work the muscles in your back and spine can make you feel energized and ready to learn. Back bends, twists, and inversions are all great for building your mental strength. Incorporating these types of poses into your yoga practice will make sure that you're working your brain as well as the rest of your body.

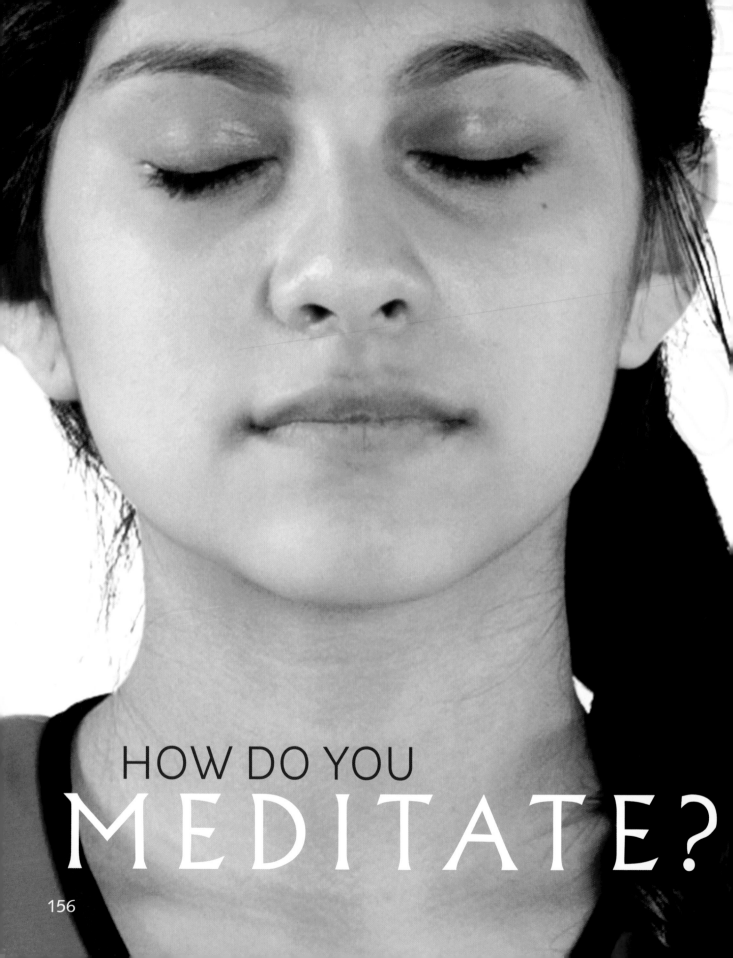

HOW DO YOU
MEDITATE?

Stop what you're doing. Now empty your mind and sit still for the next hour.

Simple, right? Not so fast.

Meditation is a huge challenge, even for the smartest girls. But don't worry. Anyone can learn to meditate. And once you've developed a regular meditation practice, you'll see huge benefits. You'll be less stressed and anxious. You will learn more quickly and have a better memory. You might even be able to sleep better at night.

There are many different ways to meditate, and all of them are valuable. You can choose to meditate on a loud, busy school bus or in a quiet space. You can meditate alone or in a group, guided or on your own. But the goal of meditation is always the same—to be very still and let your mind be free of thoughts.

Try this out—find a quiet place, such as your bedroom. Clear a space on the floor and sit in a comfortable position. Close your eyes and listen to the sound your breath makes as you inhale and exhale. Try your best not to think about anything else. When your mind begins to wander, do your best to focus it on the noise you make while breathing.

Don't be discouraged if you find yourself accidentally starting to think about homework or an upcoming dance. Just recommit to focusing on the sound of your breath. Do this for as long as you can. When you find that you can't focus, take a break. Your first meditation might last only a minute or two. After time, you could meditate for an hour or even longer.

Try not to fidget. Sit as still as you can while you meditate.

CAT-COW POSE

Cat-Cow Pose is actually a flowing repetition of two separate poses. In Cat Pose, your body will make the shape of a scared cat with an arched back. In Cow Pose, your body will look a bit like a cow with a heavy belly. These two poses work the muscles in your core, back, and neck. Moving back and forth between the poses works your brain as you concentrate on keeping proper form.

step 1 Start on your hands and knees. Make sure your knees are directly under your hips, and your hands are directly under your shoulders.

step 2 Spread your fingers wide. Press all parts of your palms down in to the mat, and straighten your elbows.

step 3 As you inhale, drop your belly button down toward the mat, and lift your gaze. Send your tailbone up. This is Cow Pose.

step 4 As you exhale, pull your belly button in toward your spine as you point your tailbone down toward the floor. Tuck your chin into your chest, and press your shoulder blades away from one another. Lift the center of your back up into Cat Pose.

step 5 As you inhale, repeat step 3. As you exhale, repeat step 4. Do this at least five times. Try to make each movement last as long as each breath.

EXTENDED PUPPY POSE

Sanskrit Name: *Uttana Shishosana*
Pronounced: OOH-tah-nah sheesh-oh-SAH-nah

Have you ever seen a dog wake up and stretch, sticking its tail in the air? In this pose, you'll imitate Fido's favorite stretch. Extended Puppy Pose will energize the spine, neck, and arms and get blood flowing to your brain.

step 1 Start on your hands and knees. Make sure your knees are directly under your hips. Tuck your toes under.

step 2 Walk your hands about one handprint forward. Try to press all parts of your palms down into the mat equally.

step 3 Point your tailbone up as you bring your forehead to the mat. If you aren't able to comfortably rest your forehead on the mat, rest it on a folded blanket.

Yoga blankets are thick, soft props that can be useful in many different poses. Folded, rolled, or laid flat, yoga blankets can be used to make poses easier or more comfortable. Fold a yoga blanket into a long rectangle and place it under your forehead in Extended Puppy Pose for a slightly easier version of this stretch.

step 4 Allow your belly to gently fall toward the mat until you feel a slight back bend.

step 5 Hold for a few breaths. Then return to hands and knees to rest.

Keep a straight line from your hip to your knee.

REVERSE NAMASTE

Reverse Namaste is an excellent stretch for your shoulders, neck, and mind. Yes, you read that correctly. A yoga pose can stretch your mind! First you need to focus your mental energies on finding this position correctly. Then you'll need to work hard to stay focused as you breathe deeply and sit peacefully in this pose.

step 1 Sit on your mat with your shins crossed comfortably. Rock briefly from side to side until you have evenly distributed your weight across both sides of your bottom.

step 2 Straighten your back by lifting the crown of your head straight up. Lift your chin slightly to make your jaw parallel to the floor.

step 3 Bring both arms out to your sides with your palms facing down. Drop your shoulders away from your ears.

step 4 Bring your palms together behind your back with your fingertips pointing up. Pull your hands upward until they are between your shoulder blades. Try to press all parts of your hands together.

step 5 Hold for a few breaths.

If bringing the palms together is too difficult, try making two fists and pressing the knuckles of each hand together.

Mudra

Pronounced: MOO-drah

From the root *mud* which means "joy" and *ra*, which means "to give"

Mudras are special hand positions. Some people believe that mudras help people to hold the source of their energy. One of the most common mudras is called anjeli mudra. It is performed by placing the palms together in front of the heart with the fingers pointing up.

EASY POSE

Sanskrit Name: *Sukhasana*

Pronounced: soo-CAWS-ah-nah

Easy Pose is a great pose for when you meditate. Think carefully about your alignment in this pose. Don't allow your body to slouch or lean forward.

step 1 Sit on your mat or a folded yoga blanket. Rock from side to side briefly to make sure you are resting evenly on both sides of your bottom.

step 2 Cross your shins and allow your knees to fall out to the sides. Relax the muscles in your feet until the outer edges of your feet rest onto the mat.

step 3 Allow your hands to rest comfortably on top of your thighs. You can rest your hands palm-down on your thighs. You could also have your palms facing up with your fingers in a mudra, or special position. One common mudra used in this pose is to have your index finger and thumb touch, with the rest of your fingers extended down. Drop your shoulders away from your ears.

step 4 Sit up very tall with your back as straight as possible. Make sure your shoulders are above your hips. Lift your chin slightly so that your jaw is parallel to the floor.

step 5 Hold for at least one minute.

 Don't let the name of this pose fool you! Easy Pose is actually quite difficult to hold. It works the muscles in your neck, back, and abdomen.

REVOLVED WIDE-LEGGED FORWARD FOLD

Sanskrit Name: *Parivrtta Prasarita Padottanasana*
Pronounced: par-VREE-tah prah-sah-REE-tah pah-doh-tah-NAHS-ah-nah

Are you feeling down or bored? Give yourself a healthy head rush to perk right up. The muscles in your legs, feet, and back will get a great workout too.

step 1   Stand at the front of your mat.

step 2   Take a big step out to the right so that your feet are at least 3 feet (1 meter) apart. Have your toes slightly closer together than your heels.

step 3   Bring your hands to your hips.

step 4   Put a slight bend in your knees and bend at the hips to fold forward.

step 5   If you can, slowly straighten your knees. If this feels too intense, keep a slight bend in your knees.

step 6   Bring your right hand down to the mat directly under your heart. Straighten your right elbow.

step 7   Reach your left arm straight up into the air.

step 8 Keeping your hips level to the ground, twist your upper body open to the left. Try your best to stack your left shoulder above your right so that they form a vertical line.

step 9 Hold for a few breaths.

step 10 Repeat on the other side.

FISH POSE

Sanskrit Name: *Matsyasana*

Pronunciation: mot-see-AHS-ah-nah

According to an ancient Indian text, Fish Pose is called the "destroyer of all diseases." While it may not cure every disease, practicing this pose regularly will certainly help put you in the right state of mind. This pose stretches and strengthens the muscles in your neck, abdomen, and arms. It also places your heart above your head, which helps more blood reach the brain.

step 1 Lie on your back. Bend your knees up and rest your feet on the mat.

step 2 Lift your hips slightly off the mat and slide both hands, palms facing down, underneath your bottom. Bring your bottom down on top of your hands.

step 3 Keeping your elbows and forearms close to the sides of your body, lift your upper chest and head away from the mat. Imagine someone is lifting you up from the center of your chest.

step 4 Release your head backward. Either let it hang while you look behind you, or allow the top of your head to rest onto the mat.

step 5 One at a time, straighten your legs out in front of you. Flex your feet and keep your thighs squeezing toward one another.

step 6 Hold for a few breaths.

step 7 To release from this pose, lift your head away from the floor by looking up. Slowly lower your back and head down onto the mat.

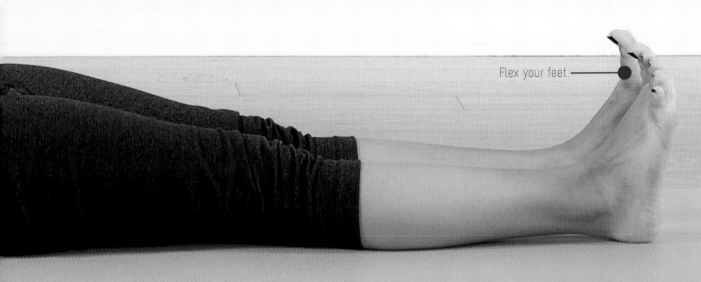

Flex your feet.

LOGS ON FIRE POSE

Sanskrit Name: *Agnistambhasana*

Pronunciation: ah-nee-stahm-BAHS-ah-nah

When you are in the correct alignment in this pose, your shins are stacked on top of each other, just like two logs in a fire. This pose is an excellent stretch for the hips and will also energize the spine, neck, and brain.

step 1   Sit in Easy Pose with your right shin crossed in front of your left.

step 2   Bring your left ankle on top of your right knee. Flex your left foot to point your toes directly in front of you.

step 3   Inch your right ankle forward on the mat so that it is directly under your left knee. You might need to reach down and use your hands to help move it into the right position. The bones of your shins should be parallel to one another. Flex both feet.

step 4   Lift the crown of your head to sit up very straight. Lift your chin slightly to make your jaw parallel to the floor.

step 5   Bring your fingertips to the mat on either side of your hips. Hold for a few breaths.

step 6   Repeat on the other side.

Flex your feet.

Keep your
shins parallel
to the floor.

171

HEAD-TO-KNEE POSE

Sanskrit Name: *Janu Sirsasana*

Pronounced: jah-NOO sheer-SHAHS-ah-nah

Head-to-Knee Pose combines a deep forward fold with a hip stretch. It lengthens the muscles in your legs, but also helps you to relax the muscles in your neck, back, and shoulders. Releasing tension from these muscle groups can help you feel focused and ready to learn. Remember not to lock your knee while doing this pose. Locking your knee can lead to overstretching and possibly injuring your muscles.

step 1 Sit on your mat with both legs extended in front of you.

step 2 Bend your right knee and pull the sole of your right foot into the inside of your left thigh. Allow your right knee to fall out to the right. If this feels like too much of a stretch, allow your right thigh to rest on a yoga blanket or a pillow.

step 3 Flex your left foot to point the toes straight up.

step 4 Sit up very tall. Center your upper body over your extended left leg by pointing your belly button at your left knee.

step 5 Keeping your hands on either side of the left leg, start to walk them forward toward your left foot. Stop when you feel the stretch.

step 6 Hold for a few breaths.

step 7 Repeat on the other side.

Flex your foot.

SUPPORTED HEADSTAND

Sanskrit Name: *Salamba Sirsasana*

Pronounced: sah-LAHM-bah seer-SAHS-ah-nah

Feeling drowsy? Homework got you down? Instead of reaching for an energy drink, try an inversion instead. Inversions such as the Supported Headstand are yoga poses that bring your head below your heart. Doing an inversion for just a few breaths can give you a healthy jolt of energy.

step 1 Bring your mat to a clear, empty wall. Don't choose a wall that has windows or anything hanging on it that you might break or knock down.

step 2 Come to your hands and knees facing the wall.

step 3 Bring your elbows down onto the mat, shoulder-distance apart. Interlace your fingers. Your knuckles should be a few inches from the wall.

step 4 Tuck your toes under and lift your knees off the mat. Stick your bottom up into the air.

step 5 Slowly start to walk your feet in toward your elbows. Try to keep your knees as straight as you can.

step 6 Press your forearms down into the mat. When you have walked forward far enough, your shoulders will be right above your elbows. Pause and hold this for a few breaths.

continue on page 176 ➡

If straightening your knees is very challenging for you, or if you feel this stretch intensely in your shoulders, work on Step 5 without moving on. You will still get all the benefits of this pose, but you won't risk injuring yourself.

175

SUPPORTED HEADSTAND
continued

step 7 Slowly lower your head down onto the mat. Keep pressing into your forearms.

step 8 Lift your right leg straight up into the air. Keep your knee straight.

step 9 Bend your left leg deeply. With control, spring off of your left foot to hop your right foot toward the wall. Be patient with yourself. This step might take a few tries.

Use control when kicking up into a headstand. You do not want to crash into the wall. Rather, the wall is there to lightly support you and keep you in the correct alignment. Your feet should gently tap the wall.

Flex your feet.

step 10 When your right foot makes contact with the wall, use the muscles in your abdomen to swing your left leg up against the wall as well.

step 11 Bring your legs together. Flex your feet so that it looks like you're trying to stand on the ceiling.

step 12 Pull your belly button in toward your spine.

step 13 Hold for a few breaths.

step 14 Bring your right foot down to the mat. Then bring your left foot down as well. Rest on your hands and knees.

step 15 Repeat, leading with the opposite leg.

Stay Safe! Keep pressing into your forearms when you are upside down in supported headstand. You should only have a small amount of weight resting on your head. Your arms can support the rest of your weight.

SHOULDER STAND

Sanskrit Name: *Salambba Sarvangasana*

Pronounced: sah-LAHM-bah sar-vahn-GAHS-ah-nah

Have you ever heard someone talk about a head rush? Well, doing Shoulder Stand is a great way to get a "brain rush!" This inversion encourages blood to flow to the head, neck, and heart. The increased blood flow can help wake you up and energize your mind. Beginners might hold this pose for a few breaths, but advanced yoga students often stay in Shoulder Stand for a minute or more.

A yoga blanket is helpful in Shoulder Stand because it can prevent you from overstretching the back of your neck. Yoga blankets are thin wool blankets. But any blanket can be used as a prop—as long as you don't mind it getting a little sweaty.

step 1 Fold a yoga blanket to make a rectangle that is about 2 feet (0.6 m) long by 1 foot (0.3 m) across. Place the folded blanket on your mat. Lay down on it so that the blanket supports your shoulders but your head rests on the mat.

step 2 Bring your arms down to your sides with your palms facing down. Bend your knees up and bring your feet onto the mat just in front of your bottom.

step 2

step 3 Use the muscles of your abdomen to pull your knees into your chest.

step 3

step 4 To move into the inversion, press your arms down into the mat. Use the muscles of your abdomen to lift your hips and torso off the mat. Curl your torso to reach your knees toward your face, and bring most of your weight onto your shoulder blades.

step 5 Bend your elbows, and bring your hands to your lower back with your fingers pointing toward your heels. Try to keep your elbows from splaying out to the sides.

step 6 Using your hands as support, slowly straighten your legs up. Try to make your legs rise straight up, so that they are perpendicular to the mat.

step 7 Press the back of your head down into the mat to make space between your chin and your chest.

step 8 Press the balls of your feet up. Keep your legs together.

step 9 Hold for a few breaths.

step 10 There are two ways to exit this pose. The first is to bend your knees and pull them in toward your face. Then straighten your arms down onto the mat, palms facing down. Very slowly roll onto your back and rest. The second way to exit this pose is to take Plow Pose.

Plow Pose

PLOW POSE

Sanskrit Name: *Halasana*

Pronounced: hall-AHS-ah-nah

Sit on the floor and reach your head toward your toes. Now imagine flipping that stretch upside down, and you've got Plow Pose. This pose stretches the back, legs, and neck while it works the muscles in your core.

step 1   Start in Shoulder Stand.

step 2   With your elbows bent and your hands supporting your low back, begin to lower your feet toward the mat behind your head. Keep your legs as straight as possible.

Shoulder Stand

Step 2

step 3 Bring your feet as close to the mat as you can. They might rest on the mat behind your head, or they might hover off the ground. Don't worry about where they are. Instead, think about the deep stretch you're feeling in your back and legs.

step 4 Straighten your arms onto the mat. Interlace your hands and press your wrists and elbows down into the mat.

step 5 Hold for a few breaths.

step 6 Unclasp your hands, and press your palms down into the mat.

step 7 Slowly roll onto your back. Rest for a few breaths.

Plow pose can be a very intense stretch. Remember to come into the pose slowly and stop if you feel any pain.

REVOLVED CHAIR POSE

Sanskrit Name: *Parivrtta Utkatasana*

Pronunciation: par-VREET-ah ooht-kah-TAHS-ah-nah

Energizing the muscles around your spine is a sure way to wake up your brain. The deep spinal twist in Revolved Chair Pose stretches the muscles in your neck, core, and back too. Feel free to make this pose as challenging as you want by adjusting the amount you twist.

step 1 Stand at the top of your mat with your big toes touching and your heels slightly separated.

step 2 Bring your palms together in front of your heart.

step 3 Bend your knees deeply as though you were about to sit down into a chair. Keep your knees together.

step 4 Twist your upper body open to the right. Bring your left elbow to the outside of your right knee. Keep pressing your palms together.

step 5 Look up over your right shoulder.

step 6 Hold for a few breaths. Keep your weight evenly spread across both feet and squeeze your knees together.

step 7 Return to a standing position to rest. Repeat on the other side.

If this twist is too challenging, modify it by bringing your left elbow to the outside of your left knee. If you want to make this pose more difficult, try bringing your left fingertips to the outside of your right foot and your right hand up.

REVOLVED HIGH LUNGE POSE

Here's another spinal twist to boost your mental mojo and burn fat while building muscle. Try the basic version of this pose first, but then feel free to try different variations.

step 1 From a standing position, take a big step forward with your left leg. Point your left toes straight ahead.

step 2 Bend the left knee deeply while you keep your right leg as straight as you can. Lift your right heel away from the floor so that you are resting on the ball of your right foot.

step 3 Bring your palms together in front of your heart.

step 4 Twist your upper body open to the left. Bring your right elbow to the outside of your left knee. Keep pressing your palms together.

step 5 Keep your right leg very straight. Lift your chin away from your chest to lengthen your back.

step 6 Hold for a few breaths.

step 7 Repeat on the other side.

You can keep the challenging twist while gaining more stability. Just touch your right hand to the floor just outside your left foot.

Does this twist feel too intense? Try keeping your right hand on the mat on the inside of your left foot and simply lift your left hand up.

STAFF POSE

Sanskrit Name: *Dandasana*
Pronunciation: don-DAHS-ah-nah

Staff Pose is much more intense than it looks. This pose works the muscles of your core, neck, and legs. You'll need to focus to make your back as straight as possible in this pose. If the muscles in your back become tired quickly, it means you're getting a good workout.

step 1 Sit on your mat with your legs outstretched. Rock from side to side briefly to make sure you are resting evenly on both sides of your bottom.

step 2 With your legs together, flex your feet to point your toes straight up. Engage the muscles in your thighs to pull your kneecaps toward your hips.

Drop your shoulders and lengthen your neck.

Keep your back straight.

step 3 Bring your hands down to your sides with your elbows straight. Rest your fingertips or palms on the mat.

step 4 Pull your shoulders down away from your ears.

step 5 Pull your belly button in toward your spine.

step 6 Sit as upright as possible. To do this, bring your shoulders back so that they are directly above your hips.

step 7 Lift your chin slightly so that your jaw is parallel to the floor. Hold for a few breaths.

If it is very difficult for you to bring your back completely upright, try altering this pose slightly. Sit on a folded yoga blanket to bring your hips a bit off the floor.

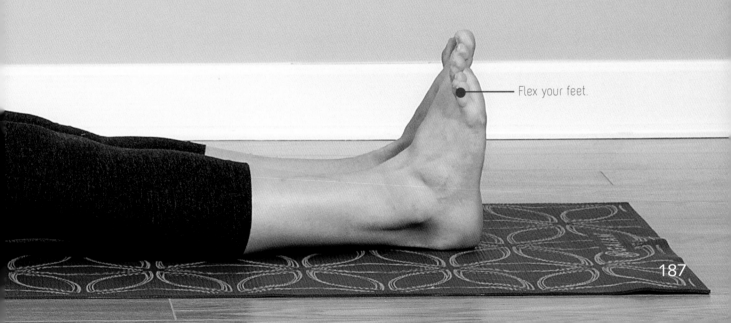

Flex your feet.

HALF-LOTUS FORWARD FOLD

Sanskrit Name: *Ardha Baddha Paschimottanasana*

Pronunciation: ARE-dah BAH-dah pah-shee-moe-tah-NAHS-ah-nah

Many people respond to stress or anxiety by tensing their muscles. When you are stressed, concentrating and learning can be very difficult. Poses such as Half-Lotus Forward Fold help release unwanted tension so that you can focus your mind.

step 1

step 2

step 4

step 1   Sit on your mat with your legs outstretched.

step 2   Bend your left knee up and pull your left heel in toward your bottom.

step 3   Bring the top of your left foot to the top of your right hip. The sole of your left foot will face up.

step 4   Allow your left knee to fall open to the left. If this is too much of a stretch on your right knee and hip, place a folded yoga blanket under the left knee.

step 5   Keep the right leg straight and flex the foot so that the right toes point straight up.

Flex your feet

step 6 Bring your hands to the mat on either side of your hips. Inhale and straighten your back as much as you can.

step 7 As you exhale, bend at the hips to fold forward. Keep in mind this might be a very small movement and you might not bend very far.

step 8 Hold for a few breaths.

step 9 Repeat on the other side.

If it is very difficult for you to bring your back completely upright, try altering this pose slightly. Sit on a folded yoga blanket to bring your hips a bit off the floor.

LOTUS POSE

Sanskrit Name: *Padmasana*

Pronunciation: pahd-mah-NAHS-ah-nah

Lotus Pose is one of yoga's most famous poses. But it's also one of the most difficult. It works the muscles of the back and gives you a very deep stretch in the hips. Be patient with yourself while you learn this pose. Focus on breathing slowly and deeply while you are in Lotus Pose. One day, you might be able to meditate for hours while in this pose.

step 1 Sit on your mat with your legs outstretched. Rock from side to side to distribute the weight evenly across both sides of your bottom.

step 2 Bend your left knee out to the side and bring the top of your left foot to the top of your right thigh. The sole of your left foot will face up.

step 3 Bend your right knee, and bring your right ankle in front of your left knee. Hold this for a few breaths. If this feels challenging, remain in this pose.

step 4 If you want more of a challenge, use your hands to bring the top of your right foot to the top of your left thigh. The sole of the foot will face up.

step 5 Sit up very straight by bringing your shoulders directly above your hips.

 If Step 3 feels too intense, place a folded yoga blanket under your right knee for support.

step 6 Rest your hands on your thighs with your palms facing up. Bring your thumb and index finger together to form a mudra.

step 7 Hold for a few breaths.

step 8 Repeat crossing the legs in the opposite way.

SEATED FORWARD BEND

Sanskrit Name: *Paschimottonasana*

Pronunciation: pah-shee-moh-ta-NAHS-ah-nah

Are your legs and brain ready for a good stretch? The seated forward bend will really challenge your legs, but that's not all. Keeping your thoughts focused in yoga can be difficult. This forward fold is a great time to work on calming your thoughts and growing your mental muscle.

step 1 Sit on your mat with your legs outstretched. Rock from side to side to distribute your weight evenly across both sides of your bottom.

step 2 Flex your feet so that your toes point straight up. Engage the muscles in your legs to pull your knees toward your hips.

step 3 Reach your arms up. Straighten your back and lift your rib cage up away from your hips.

step 4 Keep as much lift in your upper body as you can, bend at the hips to fold forward. Reach your hands to your knees, shins, or the outer edges of your feet.

step 5 Inhale deeply and lift your head and chest slightly as you straighten your back as much as you can.

step 6 Exhale and fold forward deeply, allowing your back to round a bit as you stretch the crown of your head toward the tops of your feet.

step 7 Hold for a few breaths.

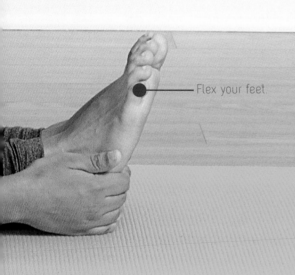

Flex your feet.

BOUND STANDING FORWARD FOLD

How often do you think about your hard-working shoulder muscles? This variation on Standing Forward Fold will give them just the stretch they need.

step 1 Stand at the top of your mat with your feet slightly wider than hips-distance apart.

step 2 Interlace your fingers behind your back. Straighten your elbows as much as you can by pressing your knuckles toward the floor.

step 3 Put a small bend in your knees.

step 4 Bend at the hips to fold forward. Bring your knuckles up.

step 5 As you relax your neck and shoulders, try to bring your knuckles toward the front of your mat. Keep your elbows very straight.

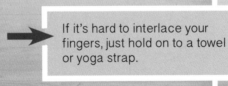

If it's hard to interlace your fingers, just hold on to a towel or yoga strap.

step 6 If this feels like a good challenge for you, hold this position for a few breaths. If you want to make this pose more difficult, begin to straighten your knees.

step 7 Hold for a few breaths.

THREAD THE NEEDLE POSE

Deep spinal twists are one of the best ways to wake up your body and mind. But if you're looking to rest your body while waking up your mind, Thread the Needle Pose will come in handy. This twist allows you to rest on the floor while you do it.

step 1   Start on your hands and knees. Tuck your toes under on the mat.

step 2   Lift your right hand and "thread it" under your left to bring your right shoulder onto the center of the mat.

step 3   Face your right palm up. Press all parts of your right arm and shoulder into the mat. Allow your right cheek to rest on the mat.

step 4   Keep both knees pressing evenly into the mat. Try to keep your left hip from rising higher than your right.

step 5 Hold for a few breaths.

step 6 Repeat on the other side.

Karma

Pronounced: CAR-mah

From the root *Kr* meaning "to act"

Have you ever heard someone say, "What goes around comes around"? You might not have realized it, but they were talking about an ancient Indian idea called *Karma*. Karma is the idea that the actions we commit in the past can affect the things that happen to us in the future. Karma is a good reminder to be kind to others and yourself in the present. It's also a good principle to remember in your yoga practice. Respect your body and muscles, and you'll enjoy good health later in life. Exercise carelessly or in a dangerous way, and your injuries could make your life difficult for you later on!

LEG LIFTS

Sanskrit Name: *Urdhva Prasarita Padasana*
Pronunciation: OOR-dvah prah-sah-REE-tah pah-DAHS-ah-nah

Stretching and strengthening your back is a quick, natural way to safely energize your whole body. But don't forget to give some attention to the muscles of your core too. A strong core will help you avoid back injuries over time, and it will also make your spinal stretches more effective.

Use your breath to flow between the different positions described in this pose. Over time, as your core becomes stronger, you might experiment with holding your legs at different heights.

step 1 Lie on your back with your legs outstretched.

step 2 Reach your arms over your head with your palms facing up.

step 3 Exhale deeply as you use the muscles in your core to lift your feet halfway up. Keep pressing the backs of your hands into the mat. Hold for a few breaths.

step 4 Exhale again, and lift your feet all the way up until they are above your hips. Hold for a few breaths.

step 5 Lower your legs all the way to the floor to rest.

step 6 Repeat steps 3 and 4 a few times.

Try to lift your legs to a complete right angle.

WHERE CAN YOU DO
YOGA?

If you are interested in building strength with yoga, a yoga studio is a great place to start. Yoga studios often feature many different types of classes and teachers. Some gyms also have yoga classes in their fitness or aerobic studios. Look for classes with names like Power Yoga, Yoga Flow, Vinyasa Yoga, and Yoga for Athletes. These active classes will highlight strength building poses.

If you don't live near a gym or yoga studio, don't worry. You can do yoga anywhere, at any time. Yoga mats, yoga clothes, and yoga props are nice, but they aren't necessary. All you really need to practice yoga is a quiet place with a flat, level area. Experiment with different poses. If something feels challenging or makes your muscles sore, keep working on it! Soon your muscles will grow stronger and the poses you find difficult will become easier.

KEEP TRACK

Try keeping a yoga journal. Record the poses you are working on and how they make you feel physically and mentally. Record where and how often you are practicing yoga. Take notes on which poses challenge your muscles, your flexibility, and your focus. If you find yourself feeling frustrated or distracted in your yoga practice, take a moment to record these feelings in your journal as well.

Before long, you might notice that the poses you struggled with at the beginning of your yoga journey have become easy. Reserve a special section of your yoga journal where you can write down any poses you hope to learn one day.

Find a way of practicing yoga that fits you and your personality. Whether it's a class in a gym, yoga in the park, or even practicing alone in your bedroom, it's important to find a style of yoga that you enjoy. After all, the more fun you have, the more likely you will be to stick with yoga to become a stronger you.

Building Mental Muscle

Yoga doesn't just challenge your muscles. It also challenges your mind. Because yoga doesn't usually involve loud music or fast movements, it can be difficult to concentrate on each pose. Try your best to keep your mind focused on your physical movements. When you notice that your mind is wandering, don't get discouraged. Just stop and close your eyes. Think about your breath and your physical alignment. Then open your eyes and try focusing again.

SET GOALS

From the Sanskrit vocabulary to the circus-performer poses, you might wonder if yoga is from a different planet. Yoga can be a little intimidating, but don't be afraid to give it a try. Start small by setting reasonable goals for yourself. You might decide to do one yoga workout a week. Or you could focus on trying to learn two new poses each week. Write your goals down somewhere you'll see often so you don't forget them.

Ask your friends if any of them are interested in learning about yoga. Having a "yoga buddy" is a great way to stay motivated. You can plan your yoga workouts together. You and your yoga buddy can help each other with body alignment and help staying focused.

It doesn't take long to experience the benefits of yoga. Many people report feeling better after their very first practice. A regular yoga practice can help you become more fit, flexible, and happy. So what are you waiting for?

Namaste

Pronounced: NAH-mah-stay

Nama means "bow"

As means "I"

Te means "you"

Have you ever heard someone say Namaste? This Sanskrit word, usually spoken at the end of a yoga class, is a common greeting in India. The literal definition for this word is "I bow to you," or "I honor you." However, Namaste also has a deeper meaning. It is used to communicate that the speaker sees and honors the heart and spirit in another person. It is used to show deep respect for someone. Namaste is usually spoken with the hands held in front of the heart, with the fingertips touching in a prayer-like position.

INDEX

ABOUT THE AUTHOR

Rebecca Rissman is a certified yoga instructor, nonfiction author, and editor. She has written books about history, culture, science, and art. Her book *Shapes in Sports* earned a starred review from *Booklist* magazine, and her series *Animal Spikes and Spines* received *Learning Magazine*'s 2013 Teachers Choice for Children's Books. She lives in Portland, Oregon, with her husband and daughter, and enjoys hiking, yoga, and cooking.

Yoga for your Mind and Body is published by Switch Press.
1710 Roe Crest Drive, North Mankato, Minnesota 56003
www.capstonepub.com

Library of Congress Cataloging-in-Publication Data

Cataloging-in-Publication Data in on file with the Library of Congress.

ISBN 978-1-63079-013-4

Editorial Credits

Mandy Robbins, editor; Heidi Thompson, designer; Sarah Schuette, prop preparation; Marcy Morin, scheduler; Charmaine Whitman, production specialist

Photo Credits

Capstone Studio/Karon Dubke, all photos except; Capstone Studio/TJ Thoraldson Digital Photography, 38, 51, 73, 94, 96, 97, 124, 125 (b), 127, 142, 144 (bottom left), 145, 146 (middle), 147, 168, 171, 188 (bottom, 189; iStockphoto, Inc: arekmalang, 203-204, Di_Studio, 205-206, mandygodbehear, 116 (top), manley009, 157 (top), Razvan, 5 (top), sparks_chen, 105, Shutterstock: arek_malang, 154, B Calkins, 7 (middle), Dean Drobot, 58-59, Lucky Business, 200, Mandy Godbehear, 1, Maridav, 12, Photobac, 157 (bottom), Syda Productions, 116 (bottom), Zorandim, cover; Shutterstock design elements/A-R-T, redstone, vectorkat